First Person Intense

A Prose Anthology

edited by

Sasha Newborn

B△ND△NN△ BOOKS • 2012 • S△NT△ B△RB△R△

SHAKESPEARE FOR DIRECTORS, PRODUCERS, ACTORS, WANNABEES

---

shakespeareplaybook.com

DIRECTOR'S PLAYBOOK SERIES. the elements of production: storyboarding, auditions, staging diagrams, budget, publicity, costuming, set design, playbill, stage managing, glossary, customized actor scripts

Hamlet   The Merchant of Venice   Twelfth Night   Taming of the Shrew
A Midsummer Night's Dream   Romeo and Juliet As You Like It   Richard III
Henry V   Much Ado About Nothing   Macbeth   Othello
plus
SEVEN PLAYS with Transgender Characters, plus Hamlet
Falstaff: Four Plays

TWO-HOUR READS

Don't Panic: The Procrastinator's Guide to Writing an Effective Term Paper.
The First Detective: 3 Stories. Edgar Allan Poe   Gandhi on the *Bhagavad Gita*
The Everlasting Gospel, William Blake   Italian for Opera Lovers. (dictionary)
Dante & His Circle. Love sonnets   Vita Nuova, Dante's tribute to Beatrice
Ghazals of Ghalib   The Gospel According to Tolstoy
Hadji Murad, a Chechen story, Leo Tolstoy

TWO-DAY READS

Mitos y Leyendas/Myths and Legends of Mexico. Bilingual
The Beechers Through the 19th Century   First Person Intense (anthology)
Uncle Tom's Cabin, Harriet Beecher Stowe   Frankenstein, Mary Shelley
Aurora Leigh, Elizabeth Barrett Browning

TEACHING SUPPLEMENTS

(Q & A, glossaries, critical comments)
Areopagitica, John Milton   Apology of Socrates, & The Crito, Plato
Leaves of Grass, Walt Whitman   Sappho, The Poems
Uncle Tom's Cabin, Harriet Beecher Stowe

TABLE of CONTENTS

Dedicated to those who dare to be vulnerable

It was strange, because as I worked on my story I regressed to my first youthful attempts at writing—painful memories of painful labor. At my typewriter, fifteen, sixteen and then seventeen wishing I was complicated. Sophisticated as well, but although my yearning for faraway places with strange sounding names, dames and mystery, I wanted it to be me, not that I would be a figure of complication—that too—but most of all that what I would be involved in would complicate me, through which I would fight my way free, to see it all as it would be through my untangling it, although I would be touched and remain touched by every aspect of the complexity including my process, and what frustrated me was a certain knowing that the things that seemed complicated were in actuality simple, lucid, and what seemed so clear was in fact so complicated I couldn't begin to comprehend it (for example, girls), which caused me to realize—in a teenage sort of realization, it began to dawn upon me that I too was complicated and yet simple not through design (though that too), but by nature, therefore others were too, and, as I continued to write, I realized that art and language were in their natures complicated, yet seemed easy, and clear, so faced with a fresh dimension in an already turbulent dimensional force, I at last began to touch what I wanted. I felt that one dimension was anger, another was identifying, and of course as always there was love and sadness, etc., but I remembered writing the story I'd found, while looking for the Owens review, and remember feeling the same frustration and unhappiness I'd felt when I was a boy, based on an innocent confusion and frustration in terms of how to handle myself in my story, and which person to use. It wasn't that I feared the first person, though I did—myself as myself shocked me—but it was also how to handle it (me), in print—I didn't know how, but I wanted me out there, in it, so, in this story I remembered, while calling myself Lucky I had made a connection with the boy-self's dream come true, in that I was at once in touch with an interior/exterior complication so real or vertical I could identify with it, and feel my anger, confusion, sadness and love etc., as a very real dimension to be in, thus to get through, and be free of, yet remaining touched by every aspect.

Fielding Dawson
from *Four Penny Lane*

Introduction to

Listen, you haven't been paying attention, We've been writing right at you for years, I brought these writers together so that you can see the difference, academic prose is dead, most magazine lit is phony and I'll tell you why, and what we're doing about it. You won't see right away but by the time you finish this book, you won't settle for the crap being packaged as literature, I mean, some books are commissioned! I'm talking about the change that some of us have been making in our writing that even we didn't notice until after our so-called experimental stories were published side by side with the best of the constructed stories. I believe in mythologies of writing, and I think we just outlived one—which is exactly why the older stories seem constructed to us. The new wave of writing that I'm talking about—face-out writing—hasn't been analyzed and criticized to death because our audience, the people who've listened, don't think that way, we/they don't read Bukowski or Grayson or Hugh Fox for elegance of structure or three-dimensional characters or plot. I am willing to believe that the age of "identifying with" leading characters was a necessary step for people during the forties and the submerged fifties. Vicarious experience—color movies, TV, genre writing, cartoons—was a central cultural fact in America during my growing-up days. The neighborhoods were pretty quiet; Al Drake's "Jockey-boxing" and "Exploring" take their excitement from the nightside, directly experiencing when nobody was looking—but during the fifties itself our greatest excitement in writing came with an intense public revulsion toward Jack Kerouac's *On The Road*. He broke the tabu. How could you "identify" with Sal Paradise, who wasn't going anywhere with all his traveling, or the scruffy unpredictable Dean Moriarty—how could you follow the story when there wasn't any plot? Well, the media hype of *Time* magazine and others on Kerouac and the "Beat Generation" squelched my curiosity for years—and when I did read *On The Road* in the sixties, I couldn't understand what all the shouting had been about. Now I think I know, which is why this book came to be.

First-person intense I call it. Not the same as the first-person narrative of the Mike Hammer or *I Am A Camera* sort, no that's the same old looking-over-the-shoulder-of-the-author "let-me-take-you-into-my-imagination" story, it's really third-person adventure ("He leaped on top of Kaldash with a fury, arms flailing and a gleam in his eye.") transformed into first-person vicarious ("I leaped...gleam in my eye."). That's not the same as me talking to you. I use this page like a letter to you, I'm turning toward you, I'm on the other side of these words, looking up from this page. I'm me, you're you. Let's not confuse things any more. That's what I and the writers in this book are doing, but it's of no use if you don't hear us.

Let me try again. You can read this introduction and believe that I'm a real person sitting in a room by a desk, because that's the "editor's desk" convention; in this case it happens to be true, I am sitting beside a desk, and I am writing to you, I am writing this introduction for you. OK? I expect you to be there, psychically, responding to me as if I were in front of you giving a monologue, an introduction to these writers whom you probably don't know. And that's what you expect of me—why, you ask, am I explaining all this? OK, here's why. These writers—I picked them for this reason, among others—do what I do in writing, they tell you their stories straight on, as if you were sitting down at the kitchen table with them, but they do not invite you into their heads to "participate in" the stories, you can't be in them; these are not stories spun out of whole cloth, they come with the wrinkles and scars that belong to the writers. Richard Grayson's story is Richard's story—no one else could have written it. The question of "identifying" with the "hero" never comes up. Face-to-faceness—I think that this change, not only in FPI but for writing in America in the seventies, means more for serious literature than any number of stylistic inventions—it's akin to the shock when Gertrude Stein came to lecture in America in the thirties, and people realized after hearing her that she'd been talking to them all along, and that they could understand her! I like to think—here's my own mythologizing—that every serious writer comes to a point where he/she must finally say what she/he means, as directly as possible. Once a writer reaches that point, the writing takes on an assurance and an excitement that's impossible to fake. Our lives are enlarged by this person-to-person sharing. Often the form of directness looks unusual or experimental, and I've accepted several pieces for this book that aren't even in the "first-person" at all!—(Berne, Livingston, Kostelanetz). In each case I felt that the writer's particularized perception of self—third-person dead, third-person bibliographic, non-person argumentative, third-person thinking out loud—had been accurately and interestingly stated—in other words, s/he had written as directly as this perception of self allowed. All four of these writers have demonstrated in their careers a versatility of style larger than simple first-person can encompass. Holly Prado uses a kind of third-person intense as a way of reaching personal truths—it's a thin fiction, usually transparent and probably unnecessary. You may be more comfortable with their pieces after the less traditional stares-in-the-face from Hugh Fox, Riverat, or Charles Bukowski. I'm claiming that even in these exceptions, the writers in this book are turning toward you, are able to say things you don't expect from a printed page, aren't just constructing stories and hoping that you like them. In some pieces you will find it impossible to slip into the writer's head, and they're not inviting you to; I find that refreshing. Let me give you some background on the problem that this book is an answer to: story. I've tussled with the problem of story for some years now, and I'm not totally satisfied with the answers I came up with. Here's my working solution: There is no avoiding storytelling. Let's work on some of the ramifications: (1) even a grocery list tells a story. (2) some person is telling the story, no matter how many mirrors or analogs or parables or fictionizing devices are used. (3) the story the reader reads is not the same as the story the writer meant to tell. (4) everyone lives a personal story over and over again, the writer merely refines it into words. I am refining my experience into these ideas—my story, as I've learned from 20 years of writing, is the struggle to express myself, expose myself—this book, for the first time, allows me to gather a chorus of voices, authentic voices, singing the same song, the Joy of Being, the Life Adventure. Even writing this intro, then, if it is part of my story, must be real. I have removed as many mirrors and tricks of language/ grammar as I know how to in order to bring this book to life; many of the writers here have done the same. Many. Not all. Not all of the writers in *FPI* would assent to this line of thinking that I just laid down; the theory is mine. I picked the writers for their quality of relying on/believing in their own lives as the basis for their writing. One result is that the only thing that binds them together is the glue in the spine of this book; no theory, not even my own, covers all the bases. The Peabody/Myers exchange is one monkeywrench, James Brown is another. My own primitive impulse is to trust these writers, as I would not trust most writers—I trust them to say what they mean, I trust their perceptions. The reality writing I've been talking about pays attention to the life we're actually living—which is undramatic, unstoried, unplotted, unthought, full of loose strings, without beginning or end. How do writers handle this raw stuff? How do you tell a story that has no plot, no characters, no beginning or end, that's not made up? I'll answer after the fact: For me, time is the clue to reading the writers in this book; look first at the writer's perception of time. Art Cuelho manages a timeless present in his piece, which is the endless version of story. The dated journal approach (David Ossman, the travel journal of Geoffrey Cook) sets up an endless sequence, which allows stories to be included. But then there's Holly Anderson and Richard Currey, whose journal entries aren't in a "flow of time." Hugh Fox's aren't even dated. The memory trip technique appears to add the story-form onto experience—compare Millie Mae Wicklund's or Al Drake's powerful reconstructs with Hugh Fox's immediate flashes, compare the flatness of David Ossman to the development and larger scope of Fielding Dawson; what I'm saying here is that people tend not to experience their lives as story while they are living them, but in the telling afterward, story usually happens (Sklar, Wicklund)—and even if it's not written as story, we still tend to read it that way. Story is strong—I've given up struggling against it, but in the tussle I learned that story doesn't have to be made up—that wasn't its origin or its power nor is it likely to be its future. I think we're coming out of an anomalous period in which the imagination has been glorified all out of proportion—in fact, imagination has always been pale compared to reality—in vividness of color, wealth of detail, incredible variety of sensation, unpredictability—just close your eyes and try to describe what was right in front of you. In effect, we've been taught not to see—all the shortcuts of numbers and names of things we learned in school are short circuits—and story is the oldest of these. We've been taught, wrongly, to take someone else's word for reality rather than our own, and it's usually someone we never meet. New Journalism arrived at the same conclusion from a different falseness—the so-called objectivity of the liberal press. The underground press, including Jann Wenner's *Rolling Stone*, and Clay Felker's *New York* band of mavericks, proved that news stories told in the first-person have a power and a depth that *New York Times* facelessness cannot match. "The test ban treaty was signed today," for example, is a typical phony non-person sentence—try to picture the event as described, with no people present! Yet this same objectivism once ruled novel-writing. My own revelation came during one of my periodic burnings—when my stack of writings gets too high I sit down on the floor and make four piles: the "important must save," the "marred but editable if I ever get the time," the "flawed in initial conception or I guess I changed my mind," and the "burn this immediately before someone sees it." At this particular weeding-out, I actually lapsed into reading what was in front of me as if someone else had written it. Pile number one, I noticed, was written in the grand objective manner by a pompous sonuvabitch—contentious, argumentative, and in general trying to prove his superiority over everyone else—and this was my "best efforts" pile. I got discouraged. Then I picked up some hasty notes written on the subway, practice exercises in description with no emotional heat invested—and there'd be occasional comments in tiny print wedged in between notes to myself to pick up mayonnaise and cigarettes, and "found poems" in my crumpled pocket notebook—notes like "Alice & Joanie at Vinny's. Not a conspiracy but I'm on the outs. A. won't talk about it." Or "A quickie in the shower with A. while Joan's on the phone. Whew." And I'd get mad at this writer for tantalizing me with these untold stories. These scraps had always gone into the "throw this away" pile, and I realized that I'd probably been throwing away the story of my life. So that's why this book is important to me, and why I think a lot of writers miss out. Writing is as democratic as third grade and a pencil. Anyone can write anything they damn please. Not all of the writers in this book are professionals—but every one of them has centered in on her/his own story in a way that I respect. I want to tantalize the writer who has not yet begun. First-person intense is the toughest exercise for a writer that I can imagine—it's opening up yourself, it's being vulnerable, it's being honest. Writers have not done well with first-person; we're still discovering how first-person female is different from first-person male—I won't go into that question at all, except to say that the first-person mode is not sexless, not ageless, not abstract. I can't pretend that face-out writing is a new school or style of writing—no, I find on my bookshelves precious few writers, the mavericks, writing straight out of their lives at us— Twain's short pieces, Laurence Sterne, Henry Miller, Jack Kerouac, Bill Burroughs, Aleksandr Solzhenitsyn. Not many in all of literature; not likely to be many. They swing a broad axe.

Sasha Newborn 1978

§

For this second printing of *First Person Intense,* the original stories are retained, with a few changes which help round out the variety of first person narratives (now including one by the editor, ahem).

On re-reading these pieces, I'm pleased with the lineup as representative of a "face out" narrative style. I had to be persuaded of the merit of this approach, but, once convinced, I believe that the real value that writers have to offer readers is—in a word—*integrity.*

May your reading, and your writing, benefit from this collection of these brave, these vulnerable, forthright writers.

Sasha Newborn 2012

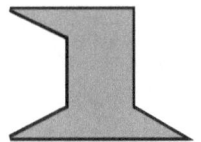

the writer

Richard Grayson
Richard Peabody, Jr.
George Myers, Jr.

Richard Grayson

I was born in 1951 in Brooklyn, where I have lived ever since. I have been a messenger for the *Village Voice*, a salesclerk at Alexander's Department Store, an attendant at New Haven Manor for Adults, a delivery boy for Midtown Florist and Canarsie Laundry, an aide at the Brooklyn Public Library, an assistant editor at the Fiction Collective, and am currently an adjunct instructor of English at Long Island University. My fiction has appeared in various magazines; my first collection, *Disjointed Fictions*, was recently published by *X, a journal of the arts*.

Diarrhea of a Writer
A Musing on the Occasion of the Publication
of My 75th Short Story

Class 2-1

Richard G.

The Biggest Bear

A boy named Johnny Orchard wanted a bear-skin for his barn. He didn't get a bear-skin, but he found a baby bear instead. Johnny fed the bear every day until he became the biggest bear in the woods. His father said he should get rid of the bear. When Johnny would let the bear in the woods, he would always come back....
...One day, Johnny tied the bear to himself and took him into the woods to be shot. As he was about to load the gun, the bear ran off with Johnny. There was a bear trap nearby and they both fell in. The bear was taken to the New York Zoo. Now Johnny goes to visit him often.

A— writing is too sloppy

I have wanted to be a writer for a long time. Miss Gura, my second-grade teacher, wasn't too good at spotting misplaced modifiers or missing antecedents, but she had a sharp eye for what was neat and what was not—at least in terms of penmanship. Today I am a teacher of bright-eyed pharmacy students. I am supposed to be teaching these future druggists to write effective sentences and coherent paragraphs. We do not worry about penmanship at all.

Mostly they are dismal writers. But occasionally I get one or two in a class who are born writers. Now that I have used the phrase "born writers," I have to admit that I don't know what it means. When I ask myself if I was/am a "born writer," I can't answer that. The urge has always been strong, often the words have been weak and unwilling. This morning, one of my born writers came to see me after class. A charming kid, well-liked, nice-looking: he's a perfectionist and wanted to check with me on some very obscure points of footnoting and bibliography. John is writing a term paper on escapology; he is a magician himself, and modestly tells me that he made over $2,500 from performing his magic last year. I do not tell him that I do not make much more than that for teaching four sections of freshman composition a year in the pharmacy school. There is no need. After I have consulted with Dean Spector about whether the proper bibliographic form requires the writing out or the abbreviation of a month in a periodical's date (an issue I couldn't care less about), John and I were talking about writing and his writing in particular. "How would you say I am as a writer?" John asks me. I think. "You're probably the best in the class." John looks at me for a minute and tells me that his teacher from last term suggested he think about going into writing as a career. Professor Malley thought John's journal entries were funnier than anything in *The National Lampoon*. Instinctively, I know Professor Malley was right. John is good. But what he wanted to know was whether I thought he could make it as a writer. "Yeah," I hear myself saying to John, "I think you could make it. But stick with it here and get your pharmacy degree so—" "—I'll have something to fall back on." Of course he knows the words. We both smile. After a second I say, "I wish I had something to fall back on." "You're a teacher," John tells me. I don't say anything.

In the afternoon I come home to find in the mail a new little magazine with a story of mine contained therein. It is always sweet to savor my own words in typeface, even in a mimeo mag. As usual, I have to fight my embarrassment to read my own words, but I find the story—for I call my things "stories"—is better than I remember it. Of course it is still second-rate, even though it gets me to laugh out loud once. But that is all right, I think. It's there in print. No rejections today. One acceptance. The editor is a sort-of-friend, but his letter is matter-of-fact. I wonder: is he taking the story because of friendship, or because he doesn't want to hurt my feelings, or because he thinks I have a "name." But that is all right, too. It will be there in print in a few months and I can get that same sweet feeling once more. A letter from Otterbein College, a school to which I have applied. I belong to the Associated Writing Programs, receive their job placement newsletter, respond to all openings for which I am even remotely qualified. I open the envelope: good rag paper inside. The letter: "It has not been an easy job trying to select ten candidates out of a pool of well over 200!" Dear Dr. Bulthaup, Vice President for Academic Affairs—the exclamation point was a clever touch, endearing. "Fortunately, we have been able to accomplish this task and regret to inform you..." Regret is all you really need to read in some letters. Often I think it is one of the most useful words in modern English. But this is really all right, too. It's not Dr. Bulthaup's fault. And who really wanted to leave New York City for Westerville, Ohio? Besides, I never expect to get any of the jobs I apply for. Only four days ago I had gotten regrets from the Chairman of the English Department at the University of Maryland-Baltimore County, the Dean of Communication Arts at Pepperdine University, and the Head of the Writing Program at MIT. I don't even give myself the satisfaction of keeping these letters. Into the garbage pail they go.

After watching "my" soap opera, I go over to the copy center downtown and have my latest story and my latest acceptance notice xeroxed. I keep a record of my acceptances in a loose-leaf binder. I keep xeroxed copies of my published stories in a file cabinet; some of them I send out to friends who would not otherwise see the magazines I appear in. It's an expense, but at least it gives me the feeling that I'm communicating with someone. "—" Very rarely a stranger will write me, someone who has read one of my stories in some little mag. Two weeks ago I received a wonderful letter from a man in Texas. "Fame and fortune are coming your way," he wrote me. "This is my first fan letter so please excuse my awkwardness." I excused him a thousand times and sent him a letter saying there were better people he could be writing to. I also sent him xeroxed ropies of several other of my stories. He hasn't written back so I assume he took my advice. Joey, the muscular kid who works part-time at the copy center, hands me back my collated copies. Lately Joey has taken to xeroxing an extra copy of my stories for himself. This embarrasses me, and Joey knows it, so this is something that we never discuss. "Have a good day, Richie," he tells me as I hand him what I owe. On the way downstairs I meet someone I sort of know, another guy caught in the English Ph.D. glut. He mentions seeing a story of mine in proofs—it is a story in the college magazine where he teaches; one of his students is the fiction editor. "It was good," he says. I change the subject because I remember that piece and how personal it was and how to make it sound real I used my real name and revealed things which now embarrass me. I wrote that I was having a homosexual affair with a student. Why do I write things like that? I hurry away as quickly as is politely possible.

At home, I think about writing for little magazines. I get out my list of stories and discover that today's is my 75th. Wow. Even my girlfriend, I think, must be secretly impressed. I must be hot shit, right? Wrong. Most of the time I doubt that I have any talent whatsoever. I tell myself that talent isn't important, but then what's left? Perseverance? Persistence? Old-fashioned stubbornness? Just yesterday I was in one of my thrice-weekly Great Depressions, brought on, as usual, by the ever-more-clear conviction that I Cannot Write. To further flagellate myself, I went to Brentano's and spent an hour going through the latest *O. Henry Prize Stories*, calculating how many of my pieces the editors must have read and—justifiably— overlooked. I glance at the winning stories and assure myself these people have something I do not. And then I wander over to my neighborhood branch library to continue to assure myself of my worthlessness. Philip Roth had a story in *Epoch* when he was 23 that got into the Martha Foley *Best American Short Stories* anthology? Maria Katzenbach, class of '77, mind you, has a novel out on the shelves?—and she was on *Today* too, holding her own with Tom Brokaw and Gene Shalit. Don't even mention Rafael Yglesias, does the dust jacket say he wrote the book when he was fifteen? And the editor of *The Literary Review* twists the knife in nicely with a pointed rejection of two of my stories. "You are a prolific lightweight," he writes, "Most of this is written diarrhea." Diarrhea. I sort of know what he's getting at: My stories are not so much solid things as dribs and drabs and noisy, brief explosions. I have no sense of plot. I use the first-person subject pronoun way too much. Sometimes I wince at my own dialogue. Nothing ever seems to come out the way I had intended it to, there in my imagination, before I ever hit the first key of my Smith-Corona.

I make resolutions. I will try to write a well-constructed Jean Stafford story. I will write less, not force myself to. I will write nothing but third-person prose about characters who do not resemble me at all. And like an ornery dieter, my resolutions make me unhappy; so I break all of them.

My friend George, who is a fiction writer and a poet, always seems so self-confident in his letters. He is younger and less-published than I, yet still he can refer to his "work" without sounding the least sheepish or apologetic. When George wrote me that I was his "favorite fiction writer," I was horrified. I'm not even a writer, I wanted to scream. Seventy-five short stories in little magazines, an M.F.A., the seal of approval from Poets & Writers—that doesn't mean anything. Saul Bellow is a writer. Norman Mailer is a writer. Jorge Luis Borges, for God's sakes, is a writer. I can't call myself that—not yet. So I have a curious ambivalence about the stories I've had published in little magazines and small presses. On the one hand, I'm proud of my accomplishments, proud of being tough enough to stand Himalayas of rejections, proud of being able to stick it out in college teaching for nearly no money, proud of the words I have written. Yet I live in New York and read the *New York Times Book Review* every Sunday morning, and I have friends who get paid more than I earn in a year for a single piece in *The New Yorker.* I yearn to be part of that world and am just as sure I never can be. But it's all right, as I said. Last February the National Arts Club held a dinner honoring Saul Bellow at which he was presented with their annual Literary Medal. I scraped together $45 for two tickets for me and my best friend Linda, an editor at *Seventeen.* It was a black-tie affair, very stodgy yet very glamorous. Malamud and Cheever were there. Dick Cavett. Tom Guinzberg of Viking Books. Real literary people. Linda and I made our way to the couch where Bellow was being sought out. She got his autograph. I opened with a halfway-clever remark I had memorized for a week, a line based on one of his more obscure writings, to show him that I wasn't just another culture vulture. Then I stammered: "I know this sounds silly…but your books mean a lot to me." I could have died; I was being so banal. And he was uncomfortable, too. We chatted for another minute about the rain and Jerusalem and Chicago, and finally I managed to get out: "I'm trying to be a fiction writer, too."

He nodded, and I practically ran away. There were plenty of other people crowding him to take my place. Standing by Linda in the corner of what was once Governor Tilden's palatial home, I felt completely humiliated. And yet I thought about all the questions I really wanted to ask him. Did you ever doubt yourself? How do you know when you've written something important? Did you ever want to give up? Suddenly I noticed Saul Bellow coming my way. He was going past me, to talk to Dick Cavett, but there was a moment when he was about to get real close. And he asked me: "What did you say your name was again?" I was in heaven. I babbled out four syllables, managing not to make a mistake. "I'll look for you," said the winner of the 1976 Nobel Prize for literature. He then passed me by. Here I am, Mr. Bellow. Where, I don't know. My writing is too sloppy. This may be diarrhea. But I'm in print, and that's almost enough for now.

Richard Peabody, Jr.

I'm your basic stereotypal unemployed masters degree holding
writer/editor. Have edited *Gargoyle* magazine since August
'76, and produced 9 issues. Presently putting # 10 together.
One of "the invisible writers of Washington." Lived in DC
my whole life. I host a radio show on WPFW/Pacifica called
Garfield Street. One of the original members of the two-year-
old Writer's Center in Glen Echo, Maryland. Worked on the
COSMEP Book Van last summer from August to October. Play
guitar and bass. Anglophile. Devoted fan of D.H. Lawrence,
F. Scott, Henry Miller, Kerouac, Jimi Hendrix and Eno. Have
poems forthcoming in *The Washingtonian, South and West,
Windsor Review, Ululatus* and *Zahir;* fiction in *Transmutant* and
reviews in *The Mill.* First book of poems is coming soon in
hardback from my friend Lynn—*A Diet of Earthworms,* and
looking for a publisher for my second manuscript—"I'm In
Love With The Morton Salt Girl." Want to settle in Western
Ireland.

Letter to George Myers, Jr.

5/18

George,
   Recovering from a troubled week…aggh…the party for Phil is a
real thing…will occur as we said on the 27th at 7pm if you're in the
mood Gretchen would love to cook you that 'one good meal'…will
be at the Harrimans on N street…exact address…3038…down the
alley by the wire mesh gate and around back…yes…should be fun
and there might be skinny dipping and rampant sex so do come!!
Shocking DC Party…arrests…massive overdoses on gretchen's
pastry/tarts…to eat and be eaten…or oh lab lab…its all cake to me
satchmo.
   Actually, coming unglued…Kevin's article about my untimely
death/disappearance/movement has been published in the *Wash.
Post*…discovered by my Dad who thought it jolly and left me feeling
weird…Desi is working on a rebuttal Kevin told me today and then

he'll write another and then I'll write from Paris declaiming my detractors from abroad in my best fiery prose...

Been reading about the life of Paul Bowles in Fez and in Tangier and am both jealous and envious...wow...he was a composer before he ever wrote and worked with Aaron Copland and did things for Orson Welles and Tenn. Williams besides which he did the first translation of Sartre's *Huis Clos* and is the one who coined the U.S. english title *No Exit*...worked with Dali...did a ballet together... amazing man and then he married the mysterious Jane who's been getting a big critical fuss lately...strange all tbis from a man who didn't know the female body was different until he was 17 and thought he was the only child in the world until he was 6!...'cause he was isolated...by his folks natch...

Ahem...back to the grind...looking for work...none to be found anywhere...whoah withs me...like woah...horse riding into the sunset...gretchen and I may go to Santa Fe...I'm dying to move out of here for a while...6 months or so...working on a bloody great novel and pissed at myself cause my prose isn't good enough while my ideas for the plot are (for once) decent and conventional with a twist...aggh...also just received a 65pp short story from Michael Brondoli that's so good I want to cry and quit and jump ship for antarctica and be the only poet at the south pole and maybe i will entertain penguins since nobody else likes what I'm doing...

Fact is I think the small press scene is a bit too incestuous for me. Seems like the same names crop up everywhere...ahem...I figure it's you and Grayson and Brondoli, Ahem and Kevin and Me and the rest of the other invisibles here who might just be the future of the east coast lit...etc....and am a bit put off by all the guys 20 years older than me who make all the fucking decisions...bitch bitch bitch...I do a lot...it just seems like too much bullshit...and if I go to the COSMEP shindig with Kevin you may rest assured that I am going to take some of these so called small press legends down a bunch of notches for my own personal ego satisfaction...

(do i get the part) I'm the cocky rebellious poet/editor...a fine madness...played by sean connery...drunk irish poet...who is a teatotaller digs Jimi Hendrix and misses him and wonders where he is now when we need him?

No seriously, I figure there's no point in getting down on all those 40 year old guys who haven't moved on into N.Y. publishing and thus (whether by choice [which they all want you to believe] or because they're lousy writers) and will never make it in the world...outside the small press world that is.

I'm an ambitious son of a bitch he says to himself. . we tiny thin guys are trouble...

It's just that there is more to it than that and that if I want to make it?? (whatever that means?? say a family and house in Ireland and enough money to get by between books), then I have to push and finally make some coin. All of which sound egotistical and awful but which is a daydream shared by many. Though it looks like my next hobby could be making movies...I mean you are not quite as near 30 as I am and I feel that twinge...creeping...that fear that I'm going to be penniless, jobless, living with my mom like Jack Kerouac for the rest of my life and never doing anything...Seems like all I really know how to do is write and spend money on magazine and other publishing ventures and spend time with the le femmes and they don't pay for that (and I wouldn't want them to)...but that's it...eat/drink and write...also a lot of hitching...

blah blah...his first long letter to me and he pukes all over the keys Nahh...just that I'm bored with, no that's wrong, I'm impatient always have been and always will be...I want it now and by god I don't want to wait...

With that the hero bolts into the night eats a pizza and chokes to death on a soggy mushroom.. . mafia plot to publish his works posthumously and rake in coins he would have never made in life... read on...

George...Come to the party if you can, should be fun if everybody is in a decent mood...though it seems that phil's leaving has given everybody that summer vacation blues and the desire to split this burg for the hinterlands be they iowa nebraska or elsewhere...drop me a word or six and i'm always this way...

Ricardo

George Myers, Jr.

George Myers, Jr. has lived in Maine, Wyoming, Ohio and
Nairobi (Kenya) and currently works for the *Patriot News* in
Harrisburg, Pennsylvania. Primarily a conceptualist artist,
he has turned to literature to find the perfect phrase. Myers'
position paper on art was recently published by Beyond
Baroque and its sequel, "On Magritte," will soon be published
in Mental Universe (Brussels). He's the originator of the
"pipe dream," and edits the quarterly *X, a journal of the arts*.
His first book of fiction, *Nairobi* (White Ewe Press, 1978) has
been nominated for the St. Lawrence Award for Fiction in
1978. Myers is currently at work and play on a novella, "The
Scrapbooks of Dr. Gikuyu," and a piece of autobiography.

Letter to Richard Peabody, Jr.

Dear Ricardo,

I'm sure we'd get along famously.... Anyone signing their name the
same as Desi Arnaz has to be alright! Thanks for your letter which I
must concur and rancor with you throughout. This Jane Bowles thing
is rather amazing. I don't understand it myself. Once again, it's not
what you are, it's who you know, and that stinks. The whole idea of
being appreciated for being a good writer just doesn't pass mustard
with most folks. For example: I made the local news on page one of
The Patriot News. People were more impressed with me being in the
news than what I was in the news FOR.
                                    What article in the *Post*? Don't tell
me you died too? You're too young to go. will you come back if I
and a few friends try a mass revival?, Sometimes it takes a little heavy
breathing to bring back our dear departed ones in the ear of Orpheus.
Anyway, I'm full of Schadenfreude in my dreams.
                                    If you can, read
through the old diaries of Ned Rorem. He got the Nobel Prize for
music a few years ago but is actually most well known for his Paris
diaries, an itinerate gossip, see? It's not what we do, but who we do it
to, etc. The orgy and one good meal (they go together) sounds great.

24

If I don't call you personally to confirm it before the 25th then it looks like I won't be down. I like Phil, a very directed sort of fellow, and enjoyed our talks together. Eventually, he'll make Ayn Rand's novels look like bent spoons. We were talking about novel writing, that is, craft (i.e. work)…I, like you, think I've got a great idea, one of two I've only ever had, and it's tough to translate that loose unsaddled thought onto paper, sentences, Weltschmerz, I sometimes think that when I'm asleep at night small but invisible sparks, like lightning, fire out of the tips of my fingers like a creative exhaust system. Overdrive. I mean, where does it all go? I'd like to go there too.

The Brondoli story sounds very good, and, holy cow, putting my name on your list of survivors like Grayson, and he, and others was generous. One must go over the edge, take a chance, on what one believes in. Who. Grayson sends me very good stuff for *X*. Then we developed a very good comradeship and he sent me photocopies of hundreds of his published stories whenever they appear which we go over, so I thought, why take a story here, one there. So I decided to do a Grayson issue of 'active interference' of *X*. He's good. Why not? *X4* out in 2 weeks. Then a special *National Geographic Issue of X*, more on that baby later. Who knows, maybe your Brondoli would be a great *Gargoyle* issue (it's tough to exclude others, I know, and WHAT WE'RE TALKING ABOUT IS THE RISK OF INCLUSION). There I go again. I can't help it. I'm an academic in the worst way.

Is that like saying I need a drink in the worst way? I feared so.

15 copies of *Beyond Baroque* were in my mail box on returning from Glen Echo last week. Probably the only thing I've written that will cause "results," as comments accumulate.

Don't worry (as I say it to you I also say it to myself, of course) about the big guys and the big bucks not being appreciative to what you're doing now. They don't know what you're doing, that's all, yet. Us little guys know what you're doing and we appreciate it. You're Henry Miller #2, which is quite a totem, quite a charm; after being hit on for years, printing himself too, hitching like you, and not getting paid by le femmes, all of a sudden he's got that house like you're talking about and saying Fuck You to one or two people besides. So the thing to do in the meantime is to create your own legend appropriately, so they get it right in the books. Live maniacally as a prologue, write when you can, dig ditches and write ads when you must, so what if it's mundane and iffy. Eventually an underground spring (you'll know it best through your friends) will well up inside you like magma, which is like breathe, which is exactly living ones life the best one can.

All else is dross.

Are you going to the COSMEP in Chicago?

Is literature a bargain?

Does it know what we're doing? Does it understand?

Is fiction a function of fact, or which?

Do we loose track of what we're thinking when we write? Do we know first or does the fiction?

Literature asks the only questions that no one cares if they're not answered.

With this, I answer, yrs.
George

the person

Riverat
Richard Currey
Holly Prado
Hugh Fox
P. D. Mackay
Ingeborg Middendorf

Riverat

Riverat, A.K.A. David G. Dailey, is a 33 year old ex-businessman turned "Mr. Natural" who has done 2 years of a 4 year and 97 day sentence for delivering $70 worth of dynomite homegrown pot...a very unnatural setting has been the turning point for a life that has now gotten a goal. We must change or we will die is what has come from this insane prison trip and all the reading...SO...a member of the Rainbow Family and a strong supporter of the Movement For a New Society...Riverat will go back to the River (Mississippi) and see just how much writing and organizing along the lines of a New Earth can be accomplished in the next ??? years. Huck Finn's my #1 hero. Recently published in *From the Bottom*, a book of Waupun Prison writers, edited by Dennis Trudell.

How Low Can You Go?

The man to the right is a drug addict who has been in this "Just-Us" system since he was 8 years old. Since I've known him, (6 months) he has cut his arm from the shoulder to the elbow, he's ran a long needle so deep into his arm that he got morphine for it 3 months till they could get it out, he's swallowed a large prison spoon. He says, "I can jump a guard, and get beat up, I can 'off' myself, (like he did in them three examples) or I can lay here and suffer. Nobody cares about me." He knows what he's talking about. At age 26 he has already spent 18 or 19 years in the prison system of Wis. "I'm doing life on the installment plan." The man on the left is stark raving bananas. He don't talk to nobody but himself. He does that all day. He fights with himself all day too. "What do you mean coming in here and giving me all this shit? Take that. (grunt) and that (grunt). Think you're pretty tough huh? Take that! (grunt-grunt)." All day the state-pushers run back and forth with their drugs to the accompaniment of "Drugs! Drugs! Medication you fucking swine!"

It's worse in the "Green-house" they tell me. That's the Hole here. This segregation unit isn't the worst they have to offer. Yet—many guys coming here from the segregation unit over in the green-house say they want to go back there. I would never—ever have believed the things I've seen in the last year in prison. And—I'm no novice to the Just-Us system. I had to come in here to find out how it Really is. I'm glad I did. The problem is: How do you make people understand all this? It's kinda like telling someone with words how a carrot tastes. You can't do it. How can I tell you how Terry feels after all his life is spent in inhumane misery? I'd like to be able to get my hands on everyone in the whole planet and slap them in the face. Throw a bucket of ice-cold water in your face. Snap my fingers like the hypnotist and say, "You will wake up Now." If they came into the prisons right now and said, "If you let us cut off your arm or leg we'll let you go home." Most all of us would go home. I am only doing 4 years and 97 days. I have 24 and a half months done now. I would do it! Can you even begin to realize what the men, women, and kids who are destined to do "life on the installment plan" would give up just to get out of here? 89 out of 100 that get out will come back. They (we) are doing "life on the installment plan"; 9 out of 10 of us are. But I still have Hope! I can still dream of a better Earth! Now do you see why they call me Crazy Dave? I got to be nuts to sit in the midst of all this pig-shit and grin! I have found out who I am. You got to get down before you can get up. It's down, down, down in here. I can go just as low as they can send me. (so far anyway) What about you? Think you can go this low? Lower yet? I'll bet that if you do, You too will cry, "Help!" just like we do. Then, will anyone hear? Yea. I know. You're not a Criminal. Do you smoke pot? I do. That's why I'm here. You just may be next.

> God Bless,
>   In struggle,
> Riverat

Richard Currey

born 1949 into itinerant childhood, navy medic with fleet
marine force 1968–72, continental wandering: back-door jobs
& sunset hoedowns. anthropology west virginia university now
medicine howard university. writing in numerous journals with
this the first major prose appearance.

from *Vietnam*

After I graduated from high school I went to work in a warehouse.
Roxanne worked in the accounting office and I remember she had
no hip definition, her hips became her legs straight on but she was
beautiful, Mediterranean smooth and self-collected, centered. I
watched her through the glass of the accounting office door, at her
adding machine or typewriter, but imagined I wasn't being obvious,
that I was subtle. On a day in late autumn Roxanne came back from
lunch and walked straight at me until she was directly in front of
me and said quietly I know you love me. I was shocked and lost in
the clarity of her stare and I stood there, submissive, absolutely in
love with her. That afternoon, Curt, my partner on the packing line
said absently Hey man you hear? Roxanne's boyfriend got it over in
Nam. I looked at Curt, stopping my crate on the belt for a moment
before looking toward Roxanne's window. She was typing, cool and
mindful, earning the money but living somewhere else. I watched her
steadily and she never looked up.

§

My hands in front of me on a bus. I never hope for anything, I cannot
tell a story, drill sergeants and bus riding erased me, one hundred
squat thrusts for losing my weapon, my piece. MY NAME IS
CURREY, SIR, CURREY, SIR, RICHARD CURREY, SIR. And the
long dead rides into forest. Swamp air lunging at the windshield. The
engines of history and loss above me. My name is Richard Currey,
sir, and the mistakes of our hands, we share them.

§

Mamasan yelling huge consumptive sobs. Lieutenant holding his arm screaming. Mamasan rocking. Lieutenant shouts he's bleeding. Still holding his pistol. I begin dressing wounds. The widow's son. Certain blindness. Lieutenant yelling to stop. You asshole he yells You never work on them. I look into the widow's face. She's staring into mine. Begin to cry. Thump of chopper blades in the long sky. Pulled aboard by the door-gunner. Then the hit. Then the dead. My head's a moon. Swallowed. By this goddam planet I can't stop crying.

§

The little Vietnamese man shadows the hootch doorway, walks carefully and lonely out into a circle of sun, arms straight up. The little man holds his arms up and looks at his feet and stands in the circle of sun.

There is a slow wind a long way up, birds clacking, monkeys cawing, the Marine's whispers, the wrapped surrender of the little man in his halo.

One Marine spills a plate of food screaming Goddam It Hold It the little man's feet clearing earth, one arm laid out in the air, chest jerking perforations body sailing backwards, falling in the shadow of his doorway.

The Lieutenant jogs around a corner and up to the hootch. Nice work he says. This little bastard is no doubt VC—must be. Write it up Gunny.

The Lieutenant drags the little man back into the sun circle, kicking the turned out corpse like he's checking a tire. He opens his Swiss Army knife and saws off the man's left ear. Blood squirt. Son of a bitch he says into the dead man's face.

The Lieutenant stands up, calls out Which of you good buddies got a camera?

§

§

I dreamed about two Vietnamese monks. It was a desert and one of
them was lame, the other blind. They lived together and took care
of one another's needs. When I encountered them I was in uniform,
in jungle utilities. They took me in, fed me, but neither spoke. So I
didn't. As time passed in their silent hovel I wanted to ask them about
an issue that troubled me. I held their silence until the desire to speak
burned in me and I yelled, my voice startling the dream: Would you
kill another being for food? Immediately but slowly and smoothly
they became trees, the shapes of their bodies the shapes of trees,
their feet taking root, their arms and heads branching and leafing and
flowering endlessly.

§

I always choose the bunks on top and against the wall. Vantage
points. Due on duty in two hours. Another masked night flying out
for the dead. Texas Sergeant and Rock howling about the wetback
bitch they banged in Corpus Christi. Squadbay nearly empty nine
o'clock Saturday night. Staring at waterpipe ten inches from my
skull. Martha and The Vandellas on Armed Forces Radio. Danger.
Heartbreak Dead Ahead. Jesus she squealed like a trapped rat when
I gave it to her Texas roars. Opens another beer. Hey Currey. Rock
yelling across bunktops You got any dope? Slide down from rack
naked fish bag out of my locker and walk up to the table. Laid it
down. Here I said. Smoke your fuckin heads off. Weird dude Rock
says.

§

§

We stand on the runway a little way out in jumpsuits. Me with
the Corporal everyone calls Rock. We dislike each other. He hates
Niggers. Says I love them because I smoke with them. Besides my
hair is always too long. War makes us clairvoyant. Watching Texas
jog to his chopper. Knowing he's through. He's over. He is killed by
a woman he tries to rape just south of Marble Mountain. A bizarre
duet dropping in on DaNang. Me and Rock on the runway. Waiting.
They come off together. She small like you'd expect. Pretty in black.
Handcuffed to the Sergeant's stretcher. His body blanched but for
the old blood where she stabbed him. The flight crewmen carry the
stretcher past us. In receiving the MPs unhook her. She looks up at
me. She spits on me.

§

I meet Lwan where she works, where I am alone at midday sipping
Asahi and vacantly watching the street when she sits down and
says You're lonely. I startle, not only the edge in her eyes but her
English toned nearly out of hearing range, assure her I am not.
When she invites me to her apartment I am hesitant and she courts
my hesitancy elegantly, taking me up the fire escape past her cat into
the one large room with the moon laying down on the ceiling and
we drink and talk, beginning to fall into the whole heat of taxi horns
and bicycle bells and beggar-chants ascending to a complete body, a
musical politics invisible from a third storey window with the night
engines of our arms and legs and the occasional helicopter grinding
past at roof-level so we wait until it passes to speak again beginning to
fall into the space we make love in, falling and unwinding through to
where I come back to her when I can and come back again and come
back and always come back.

§

Lwan, I'm captured. Standing outside the CO's door.

This man's always talkin to hisself. Maybe we should have him looked at. Maybe it's some special problem. You know, before we go ahead and crack down on him. Thank you, sergeant. Send the man in.

Lwan, it's that it's down to you. I want to turn you up in my dreaming.

Keep your voice down. Over here...in the distance, against the horizon, that smudge of emerald and rust to the northwest. Is that it?

Welcome to Saigon ladies and gentlemen, truly an America in the tropics. On your right the very lovely Continental Hotel, a beautiful vestige of our French visitors with the exquisite rattan deck furniture handcrafted by authentic native peasantry on a louvered veranda of imported Alsace-Lorraine pine. The Continental ladies and gentlemen! Home of the diplomat, the correspondent, the savant. And on your left, the endless marching. Tonight's feature is *A Yank in The Philippines* starring Tyrone Power. Tyrone, jesus Tyrone was a handsome man...

Christ it's so fuckin hot. Hey what're you tryin to prove mutha? She no free mama; I burned her tits with a cigarette, she one branded baby. She won't forget. Where you from in the world, blood?

I can't remember. I can't get to sleep. It's too hot. I might as well get up. I might as well give up.

In the long wake of sex I stare up into the violet. Lwan has put up my old rose-colored parachute over the ceiling. I jumped with it but it ripped, turning me into the planet breaking my leg. I follow the sewn tear, remembering the sense of the fall, the rhythm. Lwan feels me awake, moves her hand on my chest, begins to talk of the possibilities of my staying, being in the Peace Corps or on the black market. I am obsessed by tenderness and salvation and imagine the birds of her skep will enter my fingers at night. I am what I have lost, clocks running down in high corners of the room. Lwan is the benevolence and redemption that confuses me when I love her. Taxicab headlamps draw color across the parachute air, the artillery pops distant, nearly fantasies. Tomorrow night I'll be in the air over her country, rose-colored bodies dumped in the chopper's gut, cartoon tracers of phantom ground fire blowing up toward us. Everyone will call me Doc as though the title is holy, they'll clutch my arms like I'm a christ. And when the night is over I'll sleepwalk all over the goddam Pacific, won't open my eyes for days.

§

Tent flap lifts from outside. An MP comes in, looks at us, says You cocksuckers got nothin but cake.

Howard continues to lay down cards, I'm in a hammock to the rear with a month-old Time reading how Jackie Onassis is harassed by an enterprising photographer who tries to get her in the bathroom or sunning in the nude.

The MP turns and says on the way out You boys gotta shipment.

Howard stands, stretches, picks up his coffee cup and starts for the flap. You comin? he calls back, so I swing out of the hammock and follow.

The rain isn't as heavy as it has been the last few days: Howard stands with the MP at the rear of a military police van. Check out this shit he says to me. Musta run over a mine the MP says. You shoulda seen the jeep. I look into the van dark, see the shovelled bodies humped like piles of old hose.

Inside their air hangs rain-heated on me. One Vietnamese man, a prisoner, has lost his right arm and his pants. A sergeant looks like he's sleeping. A captain is decapitated and his head has rolled to the front of the van where it sticks, looking at me. Let's move this inside I call out, my voice clouding in front of me and I lean for support and my hand goes through the sergeant's shirt into his gut that's still warm and the darkness of him freezes around my hand, jerking awake from a nightmare, pushing my arm out from me to the night, folding back a sleeve to reach blind into black, acidic water, the man's fluids bubbling in the pockets of my fingers and sending one short gut-moan for the bad light the explosion let in, and I lift my hand out covered with his holy blood and shit.

I look at Howard. It's raining into his coffee cup, coffee splashing to his thumb and wrist. The MP is nodding like someone who disapproves. Man he says You shoulda seen that jeep.

§

§

I recline nude on this bed that is too small. I turn my head and watch
the second hand move. I am in the process of forgetting my name.
A strange church hovers above me and I remember an actor who
called it a church of the heart and said the choir was on fire. In the
pews various colorful beasts watch the blaze calmly. In the rear a
very handsome gorilla and an Oriental prostitute have lit candles and
dance sadly to the Victrola. I move in the aisles chanting Remember
John Dillinger. Prairie fires. The Invention of Firearms. The Rise
ofMussolini. Remember Burlesque in The Twenties, Who was that
woman I saw you with last night? That was no woman, that was my
knife. Remember The Lusitania. Yellow fever. Those old postcards
of Leprosy In The Congo. Remember my uncle who showed around
yellowed snapshots of the best friend he killed in a hunting accident
in 1932. Maestro! Music please! My mother is about to dance the
spotlight dance with a young man in uniform. Hats off please. I am
in the process of forgetting my name.

§

Dear Mother,
   I'm finally back on my feet. Has it been a long time? I think there
was a long time in darkness, when I kept thinking of floating over a
planet and being sucked into its face, like watching a kiss coming. I
remember, before we dived from the plane the navigator said They
won't even have time to wipe their asses where we're letting them
off. He didn't think anybody heard him. I don't know why I did.
One of the company fell past the wet air like a stone, the parachute
objecting. That night I tried to sleep on an ammo chest in one of the
harshest storms we knew. For some reason, I thought a ceremony
was necessary. Now they let me up twice a day and I walk around
the hospital grounds. Standing at the back door of the emergency
room I saw a black girl with blood on her face surrounded by white
coats, before a nurse saw me and swung the door closed. I rode the
elevator embarrassed and silent in my government-issue seersucker
bathrobe standing beside a bald priest, thinking of the bay below the
hospital, wanting weather to domesticate my skin. Once I wanted
to say something true about love. In the lobby The Godfather is on
television. It's the scene where a man is machine-gunned from a
barber chair as an infant is christened.

Love from your son

Holly Prado

I have three books out: *Nothing Breaks Off at the Edge* (New Rivers Press, New York, 1976); *Feasts* (Momentum Press, Los Angeles, 1977); and *Losses* (Laurel Press, Los Angeles, 1977). My poems, prosepoems, and autobiographical fiction have appeared in about twenty magazines, including *The American Poetry Review*; *Ms. Magazine*; and *The Paris Review.* A long manuscript, "Novels About England and France," has recently been excerpted in three Los Angeles magazines: *Momentum 9–10; Bachy 9*; and *rara avis*. In September, 1978, *Bachy 12* will publish an interview with me (done by Lee Hickman, the poetry editor of Bachy) and a large chunk of my recent work. I live and work in Los Angeles, and feel connected to the city streets, the ocean, Griffith Park Observatory, my nightly dreams, plants, and a few close writer friends whose support keeps me going.

Climate: A Letter for Harry

The long drive. The long evening. A car, a moon, this coming home to go to bed without washing my face. Summer. No socks. Your tall body around me as the moon approves. You want to talk and talk. There's a moment when either of us might get up to eat something or to drink one more glass of wine. That becomes staying where we are. Your mouth passes into my mouth into every mouth into the rhythm of the highway that we've just abandoned. To be home. To have turned off the headlights. And now you say that sometimes you only talk about things because you're afraid. As we turn our mouths to each other, we share all danger: the sudden death of cats not fast enough to get out of the way; the vicious intruder who holds a knife to our throats while he takes what he wants. We give ourselves up to fear and kiss it into even more risk. We enter the first full summer we will spend together. Drownings could occur. But the moon controls the tides, and there's more grace in her than we realize. Her rising

first quarter tonight has been as honest as my bare feet, as honest
as your whispering to me, "Don't go to sleep yet. I'm lonely." I will
never know how we can be lonely when there is so much love, but I'm
lonely, too, thinking of the few more years before I lose my fertility
completely. A long drive and its ending, its way of stopping in front
of the house. I delight in this bed. I choose the color of the sheets to
please you. We wrap ourselves in them and we whisper and we make
love in the sound of the wordless moon. How have we learned the
courage to feel under the wheels of the car, to feel into each other's
bodies—touching heart, bone, cells? How have we gained the power
to say, "I'm afraid. I talk of things because I'm afraid"? Suddenly, we
begin to laugh at how happy we are, and you get up, and you come
back, and you half-sit in bed while I put my head on your belly and
really do fall asleep. Last night, there was so much gusty wind that
it sounded like gunshots. Tomorrow morning, the first thing we hear
will be a man in the neighborhood, who's crazy, shouting, "So you
lost your three dollars! So you lost your three dollars!" We will make
love again, then. We will help the early hours ease into the room
along the bamboo shades that anyone might see through if he tried
to look between the slats. We will taste the same mouths we had last
night, remembering that we didn't die on the freeway. Summer. Open
shirts. The ocean comes, with its knowledge of how months roll to
one side, then to the other. Oh, Harry, let us always be afraid. There is
so much to live for when we know the possibilities.

Traffic

I want pockets. my hands need to curl and lean. there have been
strangers in the past few weeks: men who have that look of
wondering about me. there are things I don't know how to tell—that
I watch the mirror for the end of summer/a return to warm clothes.
why am I being held by someone's arm as I cross the street—an arm
I've just met, that might either push or guide me?

I search the stores for pockets. some sweaters have them, just at the
right length, close to the hips, so I can burrow my hands in them, feel
the soft wool give a little. it's reachable pockets I want, without much
in them. maybe a handkerchief, folded. or a piece of hard candy
that I can take out, suck, put back in the wrapper/in the pocket.
something to last all day.

and there's been an argument with a friend who's a lover who's not
a lover who might be and always has been and never was. it went on
for a whole morning and afternoon, between our houses, over the
phone, in his kitchen. both of us dressed up because other people
were coming, and there was some need to hurry. it was settled with
our holding each other for a minute, but that didn't make us forget
how long we've known each other and not at all. arguments don't
heal, even when they're about giving up something that's ready to be
lost. it's been several days. I still turn him in my head like dice/like a
revolving door.

pockets are rooms. pockets should be of matching material. I fall
asleep thinking of them: there are ways to make them and I wonder
what's in my closet. extra cloth. I must ask someone I know who
sews.

as I sleep, I dream that I'm a werewolf. I feel myself caught, going
under, losing my senses. this is frightening, because I can kill
someone, but pleasurable, too. a great fog in my body, a return to
some deep state of aggression and submission. this stays in my
stomach as I wake up. it's the middle of the night. I have never been
the werewolf myself before.

it is always about who is hunted! where we leave our trails. it is the story of trips from here to there and what we bring back is never the solution. I live in a combination of alleys, stairways, ripe flowers under a face that promises little, but I never know until I risk the open door the open legs the vision of shattering glass. that argument with my friend has the odor of what's been left too long, and its weight is too heavy to be balanced on either side. the men who look at me and wonder about me are my own curiosity. these strangers are accidents. they wait to happen, and they will.

finally, I do buy a jacket. something for fall, to wear as the days get colder. its pockets feel like valleys, the land between hills, the ability to see what's with me as I walk. pockets are not gamblers. no wheels to be caught under.

Hugh Fox

Currently on banana-papaya-bamboo island off Brasilian coast
writing novel about The Sexes and all varieties and philosophies
thereof called "Shaman: a Journey into the Heart of Negative
Capability," most recent NY book *First Fire: an Anthology of
South American Indian Myths* from Anchor Books, soon out
Almazora 42, a book of poems from Spain (title = my address
while living there) (in Valencia), to be published by Laughing
Bear Press, then *Collected / Selected Poetry* ed. by Paul Foreman,
from Thorp Springs Press, then *Mom / Honeymoon* either out
from December Press Chicago or Pocketbooks. I am 46, a Full
Professor in the dept. of American Thought and Language
at Michigan State University, my next major life-event is
DEATH...

Baby Blue Still

She couldn't have been/wasn't young, nor sleek/boney, just "subtle,"
vaginal-yoga—and all the rest too, the Yoga of Erect Nipples and
the Subtle Fanny (was taking a shit Yoga too?). "Let the Pope out
of you," she said, yogaing her hand up from his anus, around his
scrotum, as if she were praying LET IT BE, LET IT BE, LET IT BE, "you are
The Beast, the Inquisition's dead, orthodoxy is all the worn-at-the-
edges hung-tight voyeuristic jock-cowboys watching for a polite pinch
the minute they step out of line, let loose in there with me, you're
the Cat, the Ardent Dog (lips around his ding-tip), you're mad with
passion, it all is Le Combat, you've got to subdue me...." giving him
a bite that hurt and backing over into a corner, cowed, afraid, *please,
Machote, don't garrot me*, and he squirrelishly got up, "Only it's not a
screen," he said, "all this light...and I'M what you're reacting to...."

Paradise Means a Wall Around a Garden

"You've gotta see Eleanor's Poitiers for what it really was," Poppy said to Little Meg, "the first center of Women's Lib in the western world, civilized, refined, feeling-oriented, almost oriental in its concentration on furs, jewelry, gloves, combs, *bliauds*, which were tight-fitting-top tunics with long loose skirts and long sleeves like classical Chinese dancers...I mean there was this courtly woman-dominated South of France and the North—including England—with its beards and swords and nobody washing, the law of the goddam jungle..."

"And what happened to Eleanor?" asked Meg.

"In 1173 her husband, Henry II of England, came to Southern France and broke the whole party up, brought Eleanor as a prisoner back with him to England and stuck her in Salisbury Tower...," said Poppy looking at Meg's Coat of Arms over the fireplace (a swan superimposed on a castle, superimposed on a red rose, with the motto under it "Belhs m'es l'estius e l temps floritz"—summer and blossom-time are pleasing to me) put up the volume on the stereo (Angel Record 35888, Victoria de Los Angeles, SPANISH SONG OF THE RENAISSANCE, with the Ars Musicae) trying to drown out the hard-rock stereo across the street, four bronze bodies bronzing under the May 4th beer-can sun.

Severe Mental Depression

Him taking a piss, IT lingered in a shadow at the far end of the MENS, and then walking out by the river, the trees exhaling their heavy, moist midwest summer breaths, somehow IT got inside the heavy green breathing, and when he laid himself down to rest that night IT hung in the air-conditioned air over his bed: WHY BOTHER, WHAT THE FUCK'S IT WORTH, HEAVY, HEAVY, HEAVY, WHAT THE FUCK'S IT WORTH?

"It's getting to be like the 1950's allover again," his wife, strong in Christ, the first angel-emanation of The Father, said over Instant Breakfast the next morning, "don't you feel like emigrating sometimes, trying Spain? England?"

"Why not?" he said/IT said through him, only he knew you couldn't emigrate away from IT, after all, if the first emanation of The Father had fought IT and been crucified, where could he, on the edge between Nothingness and Somethingness, hope to go to get away.

Reversions

She looked like Bette Davis, I mean the big eyes, the assurance,
sarcasm, whiteness, red lipstick, even the warmth...and the
distancing,
    and she looked like his mother,
    what was she doing in his head obsessively these last few
days since the rape accusation had been hurled at him, and he
could hardly (or dare to) remember the futilely angry face of his
accuser (no, he hadn't touched her, it was all about raises and—he
supposed—her father), Mom, Bette Davis and Kay, "It's *all* about
Moms and Dads, I mean really *all* isn't it?" he remarked to his lawyer
who (cherry pit in an icecube) reminded him of his own father.

Pearl Grey

Easter Sunday, the trunk-line's busy for hours, then late (11 PM Michigan, 7 PM Heliopolis, California) the call goes through and she flowers (like a lily):

"I don't have any money for new things, of course, but I went into the closet, got out an old chiffon-flower hat, my mink stole, pearl-grey stockings and pearl-grey shoes, after I'd parked my golf cart and was walking across the street to church two cars actually stopped, a Cadillac and a classic Continental, Father O'Gorman was out in front of church, gushed all over me, and then from the pulpit no less made a remark about spring, beauty, chiffon-flower hats and pearl grey shoes...."

"How's Borgan?"

"Dead. Cancer of the bladder, buried a month already, and remember that priest that was over for dinner when you were out here, Father Carrigan? He died last week—in his sleep...that's 14 'boyfriends' I've buried now since Dad died...but I should have married Hermann. He wanted me to come to the hospital to get married. He died four days after he asked me, all those hundreds of thousands...well..."

She was a Japanese paper-flower unfolding in water, a kid's book with 'constructions' in it that pop up when you open it. She'd always been white ice and now the dark green water was up around your ankles. Walls going transparent. Your familiar house and garden viewed unfamiliarly from a balloon.

He was eight, 8047 Maryland Ave., Chicago, the perfect (ersatz) Louis Quatorze living room with the big green damask sofa, two medallions HAND CARVED! in the back—Napoleon and Josephine. Louis XIV end-tables on each side of the sofa, Louis XIV coffee table (with little metal' railing' —glass-topped, of course) in front of the sofa, needlepoint covering on solid mahogany chairs, an Atmos clock on the mantle. He was eating a chocolate ice-cream cone, his cousin Judy was there, ragamuffin big Irish eyes unsmiling as he threatened her with the cone, making as if he was going to throw it and the ice-cream ball flew off and hit the wall, bounced back down on the sofa, which didn't have a plastic cover on it right then because Company was coming that night (Maurey Greiman, his father's lawyer), Pearl-stockings screaming:

"You've ruined it, the sofa and the wall, the wall can always be repainted, but the sofa, that's the original material, who knows how old itis, it ought to be in a museum and not in a pigsty for pigs to ruin it...such a disgrace, a disgrace, a disgrace...."

Words going up and up in a spiral, hurting, his legs were going, then his hands, he wasn't there any more, you could see the spot on the wall, the ball melting on the sofa, right through him, ifhe'd only known THEN that she was/wasn't, was/wasn't, was/wasn't kidding.

P.D. Mackay

A-Metrical Techniques of a Schizophrenic is Mackay's first book of fiction. He has published three volumes of poetry: *Dead Pan, Experimental Music,* and *No Theater.* He has also recorded poetry accompanied by musical backup on CD, *Below the Frequency of Light.* Mackay lives in Santa Barbara, California

> Were such things here as we do speak about?
> Or have we eaten on the insane root
> That takes the reason prisoner?
> —*Shakespeare*

from A-Metrical Techniques of a Schizophrenic

It was only a short amount of time before the PHF Unit car came to take me away to the ward.

In the back of this vehicle I sat listening to the driver drinking a Slurpy thinking that I was going to be interrogated by the CIA. What would I say to them? Was I a spy? What would they require of me? These thoughts coursed through my now terrified body, for I realized that I had gotten myself into some terribly deep trouble and there was no one with whom I could explain my actions. My terror crystallized when I entered the PHF Unit (pronounced 'puff') where I would be reformed, or as they said there... 'groomed'.

The ward was, perhaps, one of the worst places to go to if you were losing it because everybody else in the world there was losing it too, and the underpaid doctors were not far behind. Moreover, it was situated right next to the county jail and like that institution every room had crossbars on the windows to prevent escape. It was a lock down facility, or as one might hear it, lock down 'faculty', if they morphed.

Upon entering you would think it was like any hospital with the grotesque smell of death that seemed to bleed from the place. Who knows what had died or if it was just the smell of molding trash, crazy people and that sterile scent that exudes from all hospitals. The place reeked of illness.

The building itself was a solid, three-story structure with offices on the top and bottom and the holding floor was in the middle. The lights in the ward were the type that suck your soul out of your eyes: phosphorescent, supermarket white lights that make looking in the mirror a nightmare because every blemish on your face shows and you acquire a tint like a feverish body in decay. The halls were clean...or more than clean, like they had been sterilized by a mixture of bleach and Raid. Hardly any plants or greenery giving life were to be seen. An office was situated in the middle of the block where they monitored the cameras and administered drugs. In the office there were nuclear radiation danger signs near the drug dispenser canisters. All in all, the PHF was a place not to get better in, but only to get worse in. It would be for me a nightmare.

The patient was lead down the hall were a woman who looked like a turtle said, coldly, I'll take him, as if he, I, were a new animal or a parcel to deliver somewhere. She motioned for me to sit down on an ugly, orange, plastic covered couch in a room where a TV hung from the ceiling and a sign the color of a newborn's pink skin said HAPPY NEW YEAR on the wall. The woman then began to ask me some questions.

"Do you know where you are?"

I mumbled the equivalent of a Campbell's Alphabet Soup of words.

"What is your name?" She held in her hand a clipboard with a paper on it that she was filling out. Some men were ripping up the carpet just a few feet away and I considered diving through the floor.

"Tony."

"Why did you call the Help Line?"

"I was in the middle of their ode."

The turtle woman did not understand what being in the middle of their ode meant, although, poetically, it had great significance to me, since somehow my current incarceration and previous one had overlapped. She made a scratch on the sheet and then proceeded to ask some more questions, which I could not answer because I myself did not know why I had been doing the things I was doing, and besides, what reasons I could have come up with would have been against policy, against the state of mind of the penal system. All I knew was that I had to find the truth and my mind swam with the terror of being in a lock down facility, amongst crazy people, and of having just failed royally in society.

I was lead to a room with a bed that was bolted to the floor at an angle to the door with a camera in the corner that could monitor me so I would not lose it completely or attempt kill myself. I sat down on the bed and looked around feeling the force of the cage, the effect of being locked in, the sort that is so foreign (as if any cage would be familiar) and pink, that thoughts, if reasonable, balked. All I could think about, or what filled my disheveled mind most, was visions of being an angel and somehow I had been caught by the other side and now had to bear Hell's concentration camp. And these are not even the right words because I was scared, I did not know what had happened, my visions were not working in the right context and calling the Help Line had only brought the law in to play. I looked at the pink walls and felt my spirit shrink smaller and more insignificant than ever.

The massive muscular man came in what seemed like minutes after I had been assigned. The man looked like a pirate. He gazed at me and cracked a fake smile, which made me think that he was a bad man, perhaps a pretending man, as sterile as the joint he was in. You're going to have to take this medicine, he said, holding a paper cup up to my face. I did not want to take medicine; for I didn't know the guy who was giving it to me, I didn't know what was in the medicine, and, I wanted to experience whatever my body was doing, purely. I looked at the pirate who was twice my size and took the medicine in my hand. The thought of holding it under my tongue quickly passed through my mind. Then, weirdly, The Test of the Emergency Broadcast System became audible, as if I was tuning into a radio. I listened all the while the pirate looked at me from some other time. Could he hear? The broadcast spieled out into the absurdity of the room, the lockdown doors, the drugs, the decay.

This is a Test. This is only a test. Please, without panicking, pull out your eyes, yank off your fingers, divest your soul, remove your hair, tear off your arms, unbuckle your knees, reduce your feet, and, without panicking, implode. Repeat, this is only a test. Please, without a thought, can all obligations, clear your will, suck in your ears, pull off your head, unscrew your torso, erase your penis, diminish your ass, and, without panicking, pluck your arm hair and lift your face. This has been a test of the Emergency Broadcast System…In event of a real emergency…Rip off your ass, repent with dick, lop off your arms, blow away your head, unscrew your mouth, divest your will, lose your knees, free your terror, eat your nose, crumble your face, suck off your toes, waste your time, demolish your doubt, invade your fear, cook your vowels, masticate your disbelief, stump your charisma, spread out your loss, fragment the present, sweat out the future, and supplant your past. In event of disaster... This station will inform you of how to reverse your decay, undo your erosion, beat the shit out of your fear, demolish your sensibility, change your mind, and, in the event that this broadcast fail, break your jaw, can your desire, slip out of your awe, and eat your poem. This has been a test of the Emergency Broadcast System. This is only a test.

Ingeborg Middendorf

I grew up in the upper class, and got to know its good (being spoiled, luxury) and its bad (hypocrisy, intrigues). I studied literature until I almost forgot how to write. I learned a normal profession (teacher) and gave it up. Publications: 1971 in Peter Hammer Verlag's *We Children of Marx and Coca-Cola*; in the Berlin magazine, *Courage*; erotic stories in *Where the Night Embraces the Day*, Gudula Lorez Verlag; in the Munich magazine *Gasolin 23*; in *Tübinger Texte*; in 1978, a poetry volume *Die Fehlgeburt/Der Abgang* ("The Miscarriage") for which I received the Förderpreis (Patronage Prize) of the Land (province) North Rhein-Westphalia; various publications in KAKTUS Verlag and *City*, both in Münster. Now I'm working on a "family novel," which I'll finish this year. I was formed by stays in southern Italy, though now I'm more interested in the north. I've no interest in America, maybe because everyone's so crazy about it. I was influenced by R.D. Brinkmann, who grew up in the same city as I did. Also important: Rolling Stones, Brigitte Bardot, my mother—the last since, but not until, her death. I would like an "alternative life" alone with my little son. Also important: Franziska von Reventlo. I am afraid that my child will never grow up, because they will use the weapons of annihilation that have been so long prepared and stockpiled. Our generation has it rough. In the face of the total threat, literature must be radical.

The Miscarriage

When the pregnancy test came out positive, I invited my girlfriends for champagne. They too should see the birdsnest on the balcony with the unfledged blackbirds. We went out onto the balcony. The little blackbird panics, hops high, falls out of the nest to the street and is dead. Then I couldn't drink champagne anymore and sent the girls away.

In Munich, my boyfriend H. heard about my pregnancy. He didn't call me up. Because I was uneasy, I called him up. He said he would have to get used to the idea and drove to Cannes for the Film

Festival. So, alone, wanting to have the joy, I bought books about pregnancy and birth, visited friends with children, spoke about living communally with other people who have children.

After waking up and feeling the first signs, my breasts getting large and sensitive, I lay my palm on my belly and sang to my developing child—it must have had the size of a thumb by then:

> my little thumbling, my little thumbling
> my little thumbling, sleep well
> my little thumbling, my little thumbling
> my little thumbling, grow large.

The doctor, a woman, embraced me when she confirmed my pregnancy. The birth should come in January.

My boyfriend called up from Cannes. He was happy, too. Everything was more concrete now, not so psychological. When I told him the expected delivery date, he said, the child must have been conceived in April and I didn't come back to Berlin from Crete until the middle of April.

Later I picked him up from the airport. It was impossible, he said, that he could be the father.

I should try to remember.

That I tried once to sleep with a guy on Crete, admitted. But I ended the attempt before it took place. H. spoke of the mentality of the southern peoples, of ejaculatio praecox, of possible possibilities. I showed him my basal temperature curve, reckoned my fertile days out loud. Only he could be the father. But the mood was heartrending, for his doubts remained.

With these doubts, which he shared with his best friends and which led me to ever-meaner fantasies, he had already taken our child from me. I had wanted to get pregnant by him, carry him in me, cradle him in my arms, call him by his name. Give him life. How I have longed for this child, I sobbed. The answer: not me. I always wanted a child from you. Not me!

Then I began to hate him. No more talk of joy. I could only flip out any more. This wronging of my person, this insulting of my wishes. this mean refusal of paternity and of the child. My God, the sensitively sensitive life in me, how it was shaken! I cried, screamed, swung at everything. Hated everything. Every thing, every person. Raged even at the air and sun. Did I still want the child—was it then still there? Didn't it feel everything? No more songs!

H. invited friends over. Couldn't he stand to be with me alone? I made scenes in front of all. Just before Pentecost holidays I went with him, more or less unwillingly, to visit an acquaintance of his who had a child, who lived in Lichterfeld in a garden with other women and children. Well-bounded flowerbeds and lawns, sand boxes. The apartments perfect, the faces panicky. The woman flew to H. with flushed face. She didn't notice me till later. H. laid himself, white-jacketed, in the chaise lounge, smoked, praised the wine and the somewhat teensy duck, puffed the cigarette smoke fashionably in the direction of his admirers. Cannes was spoken of. Film and television projects. The ladies are attentive. I grasped for my book: *Destruction of Hearing and Seeing in Our Culture* and tried to read. My appetite was gone. But I couldn't repress my agitation and rage, stood up, advanced upon the Group Portrait Wiith Gentleman and cried out: The nerve, to invite someone and then to treat them like they weren't there—to the ladies—and from him, H., it was an outrage. The whole atmosphere was unbearable. It makes me so sick I could vomit.

Trembling, I stood before the three. H. raised himself, cigarette in oe hand, the other loose on his hip. Master of the situation, in white Star jacket. Not a word from him to me. No gesture. Slow crushing out of the cigarette. The ladies watched.

Hate, Rage, Helplessness. I would have liked to beat them all to a pulp. Smashed into their stubborn traps, till the blood squirts. To have thrown a bomb and blown the whole used-up-ness to smithereens, to mow the whole lawn party mustiness down with a machine gun. But what could I do to them. I turned around. Went.

Drove off with the rattling VW. My Starfighter took off across the intersection agaist the red light. (Cries, curses, screeching tires, threats, police.)

Back in the apartment. What now? Wait. Footsteps in the stairwell. The relief was only temporary. Heart pounding, heart pains, heartache. I call up a girlfriend. Force a date on her. It is evening. We speak with each other. The talk keeps coming back to H. H. H. H. H.…. (Is he implanted in my brain? Am I obsessed? Where am I? Where the others? Where the world around me?)

At two in the morning back in the apartment. No one. No sleeping H. No cursing H. No conciliatory H. I get jittery. Telephone. Where shall I sleep. Not in the apartment. There is no one in the apartment. I reach R., who waits for me, half-asleep and in a somwhat sour mood, with his girlfriend in the overfilled apartment of an acquaintance. 3 in the morning. Guilty conscience, to have disturbed them both. They show me a small room. No curtain, desk, couch. Morning is already lighting. The heart races. Abandoned; abandoned! In the next room cuddle together two in love. My body shakes, kill the pain! But how? Tablets could be harmful. For I'm pregnant. (Am I pregnant?)

The couch, next to it a mattress leaning against the wall, it looks fucked out. On the table, accounts, bills, papers. A little pocket change. Should I steal it? Out the window I see a tree. Blue sky. Pictures: H. in the city. Already in the morning, shortly after the performance he has called up a woman. Visited her. Rung the doorbell. Looked around quickly in the hall, went to her room, took off his clothes without a word. The woman, still young, blond, slim, sits on the bed. Her long dress is patterned in a colorful green. He shoves the skirt hem high. You have nothing on underneath. Penetrates her. Pulls his cock out before he comes. Moans with his head back and eyes closed. He goes into the bathroom. Puts on Bob Dylan. Knock, knock, knockin' on heaven's door, knock, knock, knock... "tenderly" shoves a foam capsule in. They ball. After the orgasm, he sings. Laughs. Falls asleep. Later they go out to eat.

Excruciating rage. Pain. Such pain. Where can he be? Where is he? With what woman? (Heart thumping!) I would like to be able to see into every apartment in Berlin. Into every damned apartment in the fucking Federal Republic, the DDR, every apartment in Europe, see into every apartment in every continent. See him! Wherever he is! With whomever he is! See! (Speak?) Unbearable heart-racing! The breasts, are they still taut?

Is the child still there—can it hold out through the fever? Leaving early. Leaving a note behind. Couldn't sleep any more, etc....

Back in the apartment, waiting. Aha, so he hasn't come. Took off somewhere again. Or is there a sign after all? The telephone? A note? In the afternoon a friend calls up. Hello honeypot. How are you? Not so well. I believe you. H. is gone, uh huh. He called me up to say he was fed up, he said. Isn't in Berlin any more. No he didn't say where he was going. You better come to terms with it. Now's time to think it through. It doesn't work like that. You made it hell for him.

Look through all the addresses. Call all acquaintances. Again and again.

Ruthlessly, whether day or night. I get to hear phrases like: be strong. And: don't let your head hang. We don't really want to live with these crazy guys. You can turn to women too. But we want to, don't you? And can't. Am I right? Endlessly talking, until I hang up, exhausted. No one calls me up of their own accord!

A letter comes. Special Delivery. Monday morning, seven o'clock. (This idiotic heart-pounding) I open the envelope by holding it over steam. For the content is clear. And there it is. typed. clear as can be; can't, won't live with you. And not because of the momentary pregnancy. After all I'm no bureaucracy. I want to devote myself to my work. Create a new existence. First go on a trip. Don't know where. No return address. No closing! I reseal the letter, cross out my address, scribble thickly: *moved.* Write the address of one of his friends on the front and strike through his name on the back many times, angrily. The coward! The coward!

I dial the number of a friend of H.'s. Yes, H. is there, but he doesn't want to speak with you. That happens sometimes that one just *can't* any more. Blocked! I try to describe my condition. Not sleeping, not able to eat, not working. Fever attacks. Beside myself. Just one word. Please! You are stronger than all of us together, says the friend. Whoever suffers so much outwardly, doesn't suffer inwardly, I think his sentence to completion. Gretchen occurs to me: the person, who you have beside you, I hate in my deepest soul. I hang up.

I can't think about a child any more. Feel nothing any more. Everything limp. Let yet another limit of shame fall: a letter to H. Beg him to come. Just during the pregnancy. Just the first three months, which are so dangerous. Even explain my flipping out.

That night I bring an earlier boyfriend to bed with me. Even the smell gets on my nerves. Lets my longing for H. increase. Flee to the next room. Try to sleep. No ease, just panic. Nothing matters to me any more. I dial again the number of H.'s friend. 5 o'clock in the morning. Let it ring and ring. No one picks up the receiver. After awhile the busy signal. I'd like to tear myself to pieces.

I've had hardly any sleep in all these days. Sometimes, after hours of shifting around my chaos: a half fixed up, half dismantled dwelling, no trade, no man who stands by me, a few friends who I may not burden, and again and again the worry about the child—how shall it grow up, when I myself am broken by the confusion. Sometimes, after hours of restless undignified choking on this miserable crust of reality that has fallen to me, sometimes for a moment I fall into distracted slumber.

In the morning, for days now, everything limp. Only morning

sickness remains and the worsening fear: is the being in me still alive? Has it died of my fever?

Everything talked to death. Felt to death.

I make a try at working. Talk in my diploma seminar of my idea to write a thesis about pregnancies of single women, programs of self-organization, maybe a curriculum model.

On the same day, at the first meeting with the pregnant women, I feel a sign in my abdomen like my period. I go to the toilet. Bleeding. Not badly. But blood. One of the girls takes me to the Westend Clinic. Pulstrasse 4-14. It is midnight. In the clinic, first a low, then a no-longer-measurable pregnancy hormone level is ascertained. And always changing results with echo diagnosis. After a few days there, the bleedings have stopped. I am released with the instructions, absolute bed rest. Whether the pregnancy is still intact will show itself. Hoping and fearing begins. Light bleeding again: taxi—clinic—examination. Maybe it's not so bad. Or is it? My only hope is in the echo sounding. In any case there is doubt.

H. is back again. As long as it looks like I'll have a child he is from skeptical to rejecting. But the more hopeless my struggle and my chances become, the kinder and more considerate he gets around me, consoles, takes care of me, and even makes a few starts at painting a future for us: Try again. With more calm and patience maybe we'll get more relaxed and he even says: I'm sorry!

As H. has to drive for two days to K., it's clear that the child doesn't live any more. Maybe not for a long time already. Have you had any illness? For example fever, I am asked. Ex post facto there is no way to find a cause for the unhappy course. All that is certain is that I have to be scraped out. "Curetage," I shrink just from the word. Refuse. Cry. Am at my end.

I scream at H. that I hate him. That he is the murderer of my child. That in him I can now see only the murderer of my child, whom I'd like to kill. How does he think he can stand up to my hate, I weep. If any one has to, he says, then he has to bear the hate. And he wants to. H. drives away.

Now I want to walk around with the dead child so long that I die of it. That's insanity what you're doing, says a girlfriend. If the child is really dead, it has to get out of your body. The sooner, the better. Be reasonable.

In the medical dictionary I read about *abortio missio* (dead embryo that is not cast out but remains in the womb and rots. The resulting ptomaine can cause clotting problems that lead to mortally dangerous bleeding): the "extraction" of a missed abortion is one of the most dangerous operations because of the dangerous bleeding and because of the morbidity of the cervix wall.

On the evening before the operation, I gave it to H. one more time. In the presence of patients, the nurses, and a visitor I cursed him as the murderer of my child and tried to hit him. Tried to run away from the clinic, too. I wanted to die with the corpse in my belly.

The nurse was supportive. I used to let everything eat into me too, she said. I got sick. Now I scream everything out. Everything direct and don't let anybody abuse me. I know what I'm talking about. I have four children and I've had three miscarriages... And all with one man. Just don't believe it's any different with other people. They just pretend it's different.

The next day, H. was there at 8 in the morning. It must have been care and thoroughness. I experienced it as surveillance: the man who accompanies the condemned one to the executioner is punctual and friendly too.

With all my power I resisted the anesthetic, the loss of consciousness. H. stood next to the gurney. When the orderlies came to take me to surgery, H. was gone. He'd had to go get cigarettes. At my urgent request, one of the orderlies goes to the waiting room, where H. might be. Of course he isn't.

The last wave of panic. I try to climb down from the gurney. I am easily overpowered. Manipulation of tubes. Unconsciousness.

While I was still in the hospital, H. organized and carried out his moving out. During his visit to the clinic he tells of cleaning the apartment. Now I am alone. The bleeding has still not stopped ten days after the operation.

I can no longer describe my feelings when I see a pregnant woman. Nor the feeling when I walk past a store with baby clothing and toys. If I see a child, I look away.

memory

Fielding Dawson
Albert Drake
Merritt Clifton
Art Cuelho
Millie Mae Wicklund

Fielding Dawson

Born in New York City, raised in Kirkwood, Missouri, and attended Black Mountain College. Served two years in the US Army (noncombatant). Came to New York in 1956 and have been there since.

Has published widely in magazines large and small, nationwide, as well as England, Germany, Mexico, Canada and Australia, and am in library collections worldwide, including Russia.

Has written and published stories, memoirs, essays, novels, and book reviews, here and overseas.

Represented in the following anthologies: *The Moderns*, Corinth Press, editor Leroi Jones; *The Story So Far*, Coach House Press, editor David Young; *New Fiction from the Fiction Collective*, Braziller, editors Ron Sukenick and Mark Mirsky.

Books in print: *The Mandalay Dream*, Bobbs-Merrill; *The Greatest Story Ever Told / A Transformation*, Black Sparrow; *A Great Day for a Ball Game*, Bobbs-Merrill; *The Sun Rises into the Sky*, Black Sparrow; *The Man Who Changed Overnight*, Black Sparrow.

The Field

from Four Penny Lane

One winter, a couple of steps after the war when I was a highschool junior, I discovered a field while on another of my many long walks.

It was on the northwest side of my home town, about a mile from where I lived, and far enough to verge on real country. That part of town—its limits—plus the field, gave me a taste of the sky and the sun, or the moon and the stars.

Of the heavens.

The field was very large, flat, of square shape, and held Hopper's watercolor space, which is as it was wide open, and perfected in oil, took volume.

Our highschool ballfield was large too. It extended, without markings or fences, into the hockey and soccer fields beyond which were followed by two softball diamonds, a fence and the main street to town. The scale of it could be said to have been as deep as the old Polo Grounds, though not so wide in the outfield. If a ball went over the left fielder's head it seemed a homer for sure—except for Al Heinz, whose arm was as strong as Furillo's and who was nicknamed Rifle, and whom I saw throw—from the softball diamonds—one-bouncers into Tiny Moore's waiting glove at home, catching the runner whose lazy third base coach had said take it easy going in.

But the field I discovered while out walking was half again that big, and though not as flat (not having been rolled), it was awesome, a bit rough, but as neighborhood kids had played scrub ball there, home plate was discernible, as were the basepaths, though there was no actual home plate, nor bases. Distant trees surrounded the field, and beyond them in a southwest direction the hilly Missouri countryside went, untouched—a virgin savage space to the horizon.

There was no backstop.

There, behind home plate, scraggly grass became scrub brush into the trees beyond which, and down a slope, ran a narrow pitted asphalt street.

The field was so big a certain haze hung over the far outfield, which seemed to shimmer, and in a sense was the reverse of beckoning. Not that it was threatening, but there was a presence out there, and a force which seemed to exude a reflection, perhaps of outer space and the planets, as if their metals cast a glow during the day like damp iron at night. A high fly would get lost up there, and were it a long drive, the Rifle himself couldn't bring it in.

I walked home seeing it, thinking, and remembering it as if I was recalling my future.

And around Valentine's Day, sure enough you know, *we knew*, a couple of warm sunrises brought out buds from the earth and baseballs from oiled gloves and the gloves themselves from their string binding, and we played catch and shagged flies on mushy grass and topsoil above the frozen ground below, and around a collection of suns later it came to pass that the guys who played in the summer church softball league would play a hardball game among themselves weather permitting, on, no less than Good Friday afternoon when we got out of school to go to church, the where of it being settled by my suggestion of that field, which some knew about, living near or in that general neighborhood.

To justify our game as well as satisfy our need for a stimulating motive, and a generalized sense of organization, smokers vs nonsmokers would leave school, go to church for a quick prayer, leave, go home for our gloves, bats and balls, and meet at the field, the virtuous non-smokers against the devilish smokers, ah well, had things been different the Devil's fortune would have illustrated the possibility that the degradation of the body through cigarettes could produce winners, but as God gave us all fair weather that day, that early April afternoon, it was written in the stars that those non-smoking angels would win.

But at the beginning of the game, because the Catholics could in fact (haha) but *never* skip church, and Protestants being a mild and (in this sense) rather indifferent batch, depending, we were lucky to get eighteen guys, and as some of us were late, with the details and rules to be worked out—what to use for bases, the problem of no backstop being solved by each team at bat volunteering an honor-bound backup man to the catcher, and if the ball got by both, one extra base only—but the game at last began, albeit quite a bit later, meaning, to our guilty dismay, we could have stayed at church for the whole service, and too, there was our anxiety when we would get home—or, would it be when we should have anyway, had we stayed in church—but, well, the game began and as it went on, all else was forgotten and the action began to take its shape, and the dimension of energy released in skilled continuity, in that field, as plays were marked by competitive and devilish or virtuous outcries regarding smoking as that non-smoking shortstop threw our third baseman out at first remarking he needed no cigarettes to do that while a chance later when our left fielder slid safe into second he rose, dusted off his pants, lit up a Chesterfield and announced that smokers hit, and as we all knew each other, had played against as well as with each other, and we were good ballplayers, the game became well played in the unusual sense of ourselves versus ourselves, extra compelling, that certain field a spirit took shape, consciousness intensified until we baited the hits, overreacted, and linked with an intuitive perceptive inner field, a higher, more sonic order, and the game was on edge, its edge at its best, and if chromatic science's foolish ticktock's calculation regarding, in illustration, the magnitude of the universe ala *The Reader's Digest Atlas*—if it's correct that there are a hundred thousand million stars in the Milky Way, and it would take a space ship travelling at one hundred thousand miles an hour, six hundred and seventy million steps to cross that Way, I felt the rush of vast inter-stellar space around me, I felt I was in, and of vast cosmic rhythm and wind, I was in pure motion, I felt *I am a Star* as I gave

the signal for the fastball which I caught on the inside corner—strike!
called the honor-bound umpire, and I fired. it back to my pitcher,
who threw again, and then again, fastballs, curves—sidearm and
overhand—the changeups and the drops flew in to me, and the
sustained, high inspired excellence took me into a fresh dimension
I know as one of sustained accelerating concentration in space,
perhaps kin to savages on the hunt or the organic miracle in durable
pigment moving straight out into the ceaseless and expanding
universe—and yet beyond, straight out all the way, yet humble, and
crabwise no doubt, against the mere face of it, baffled, that day,
in brilliance we were, struck zenith in a boyish curse, and outcry
followed by a laughing shout—HEY YOU GUYS! IT'S DARK!

I blinked. We looked around. He was right—night was upon us.
My pitcher was a dim silhouette against the vast outfield and the
players could hardly be seen, it *was as dark as The Turn of the Screw,
as dark as Germany.* I felt a hammer strike of Africa. The throw I'd
returned to my pitcher—he lobbed back to me—I GOTTA GO HOME,
someone yelled.

I missed my pitcher's soft throw, but with the help of my backup
man—who had missed it—we found it in the grass, while others got
into jackets realizing how cold it was, and we left the field, quick,
but not without wit, and laughter, in wisecracks, jokes and puns
on the language used during the game against the language of the
game...and after I said so long to Dajo at the end of his front walk—
both of us having worried out loud—for the applecart was upset in
our visage: something was over in the complete sense of having just
begun, a bare thread of a beginning, in our dirty, sweaty, probably
wild-eyed selves, gloves and bats in hand, coming down from the
exhilaration of our journey.

Albert Drake

Poetry, fiction, prose in some 250+ magazines, including
*Redbook, Best American Short Stories, Northwest Review, Poetry
Now, Epoch, Poetry Northwest, Shenandoah, Easyriders, Rod Action,*
etc. Edit Stone Press (since 1968) and Happiness Holding
Tank (since 1970). National Endowment for the Arts grant
(for fiction), 1974. Recent books: *Tillamook Burn* (The Fault,
1977), *In the Time of Surveys* (White Ewe Press, 1978), and *One
Summer* (White Ewe, forthcoming). Born and raised in Oregon;
attended Portland State College and University of Oregon;
moved to Michigan in 1966 to teach in the English Dept. at
Michigan State University, where I'm Associate Professor. The
summers are spent in the woods at Sixes, Oregon, in a neat little
cabin my wife and I built.

Exploring

The door was open.

"C'mon," Horace said, giggling, holding open the door through
which they had passed a million times coming from the playground.
"Let's check it out."

They stood within the cool shadow of the alcove at the rear of
the school; on one side was the grassless playground, where huge
dusty-brown grasshoppers clacked with urgency in the hot sun, and
on the other side the black maw of the open door.

After circling the empty school building, testing every door, they
had found this one open. "C'mon," Horace said again, peering up the
darkened stairway as if it were the abandoned fort in Beau Geste.

Chris looked around the serrated cement column and listened—
the empty streets, the dusty playground, grasshoppers—and then he
turned and entered the school.

The stairwell was dark and they waited until the familiar objects
materialized: the oak bannister, the narrow tongue-and-groove
panelling, the foot-worn steps. The school had been in use for over
fifty years, and soon it would be demolished.

As he followed Horace up the half-flight of stairs, barely

breathing, Chris thought *how familiar everything was!* Nine years spent in this building! Now empty, the place was not much different from when it had been full. Along the side and main halls hung the paintings which had once terrified him: George Washington materializing from the clouds, Roman columns, a pastoral scene of semi-clad picnickers in Olden Days, head shots of stem, unforgiving old men.

The slightest noise echoed against the wooden walls, and Chris was sure he could hear the echo of his pounding heart. The halls smelled of sawdust and linseed oil; how many times had he seen Johnny Johnson ("Yonny Yonson"), the janitor, spread against the oak boards to clean up a kid's vomit? They stood in the darkness of the main hall, dark at two on a brilliant summer day, and darker than anyone could imagine on a rainy winter day.

Inside, the school was both scarey and comfortable. He remembered how after one had arrived at the school one was held in the warm classrooms and protected against wind and rain. Many days he had felt the school was cozy; the poor old cafeteria always spouted forth the delicious odor of hot, homemade tomato soup; the poor old auditorium with its folding wooden chairs brought them together for songs and Christmas plays and sometimes a flickering movie showing Sinbad or Gulliver.

They wandered downstairs and into the gym, whose cement floor had the chill of winter. How many teeth had been chipped or broken on that cement? he wondered, probing with his tongue his own partially missing front tooth. They cautiously pushed open the door to the boys' john, with its strange labyrinth of tall water reservoirs and pipes. Here Bobby Meersham had fallen while jumping from pipe to pipe and had fractured his skull; perhaps, Chris thought, that accident was what had made him a little nutty.

Back upstairs they wandered into familiar rooms and ones they had never entered in all the years between kindergarten and eighth grade: the teachers' room, and the large cubby hole where Mrs. Van Dant kept all the musical instruments. Most rooms were empty, but in the office of Mr. Buffon, the principal, they found two ink bottles. Slowly and with great care Horace opened the caps and dribbled ink across the desk. Then he stood back and giggled.

The action triggered some escape valve: not only would they never have to return to this school, the building wouldn't be here in a few months. Therefore, it was perfectly okay to have their revenge against all the hours they had lived within the confines of these walls, the long afternoons in boring classes when they could have been playing at Indian Rock, the hours they had had to stay after school for some minor infraction of the rules, to write upon the blackboard two hundred times "I will not infringe upon the rights of my neighbors" when they could have been sailing rafts along Johnson Creek or hiking up Mt. Scott.

In the main hallway Chris removed the big brass fire extinguisher from its hook and upended the cylinder; a stream of liquid played across the plaster and wood walls, the window with Mr. Buffon, Principal painted on it in black letters, the chairs, and as he walked into the room to spray the chest-high wooden partition behind which the secretary, Mrs. Edgington, had always sat, the liquid slowed to a trickle. Chris shook the container, and dropped it in the corner.

They went from room to room spraying the fire extinguishers on everything. They wrote obscene words in liquid on the blackboards. In the room Chris had once had as an Art room the extinguisher refused to work. He shook it, but nothing came out. Then he unscrewed the entire top and found a gray container attached to it. He pressed a finger against it, and suddenly liquid sprayed across his face. It was sharp, biting; he knew the extinguishers worked on the soda-acid principle, and he realized that this was the acid. Throwing away the container, he jumped back and hollered, his eyes closed, afraid to open them and afraid to rub them with his hand.

"What the heck?" Horace said, laughing.

"Acid!" Chris said, rubbing his shirt sleeve against his cheek and eyes, spitting the bitter taste which had entered his mouth. He blinked, found he could see, and began to laugh. "I gotta get some water."

The only drinking fountain in the entire school was in the basement, and they went there to wash off the acid. Chris leaned his burning cheek into the trickle and as the coolness washed over him he thought of wet wool jackets and boot socks, the oily odor of yellow rain slickers, of standing safety-patrol in the near-darkness, sack lunches, the corrugated cardboard sheets on which he had taken brief naps in kindergarten, chalk dust, overalls and corduroy, the slick paper of new books, erasers, playing marbles in the muddy ground of spring, looking out the window when the weather was too beautiful for any school day.

"C' mon," Horace called. He was hauling a large block of wood away from Johnny Johnson's furnace room and up the stairs. Chris grabbed one end and they took it to the first floor; Horace lifted the block, rocked his weight back and forth, and let it fly: slowly it tumbled through the air and in slow motion crashed into and past the glass doors which led to the false balcony. Within the empty building the noise of falling glass echoed endlessly, as if each splinter shattered into sound.

"Oh christ," Chris said, moving back, "somebody's going to hear that."

Horace laughed. "Give' em a broadside, clear the decks with grape-shot!"

They shot off more fire extinguishers and broke up chalk. Chris found a rock on the floor of Mrs. Douglas's room, lying where it had fallen after it had sailed through the window, and threw it into the blackboard. He picked it up and threw it again. After he had made several holes in the board he threw it overhand at a ceiling light; it hit the base and the heavy glass fixture crashed intact to the floor where it disintegrated. Chris started to pick it up again, then stopped.

"You hear something?"

They stiffened, listening; the empty halls were silent. However, not wanting to be caught in a room they wandered down the hallway to where the main halls intersected. They listened, poised against a silence which was so intense it seemed to have a solid weight. Chris heard the beat and echo of his heart. Horace giggled, shrugged, and walked toward the principal's office; he picked up an empty fire extinguisher cannister, raised it overhead, saying, "Death to the infidel!" and was about to throw it through the opaque window when heavy steps sounded along the boards.

"Run!" Chris said, trying to make his legs move as he saw beyond Horace a figure coming around the corner, saw the blue uniform of a fireman, saw Horace drop the cannister with an awkward, almost feeble, motion and turn to begin to run, and then his own legs were moving, his feet slipping against the oak floor. J eezus! he thought, scared and thrilled at the same time, running from the shadows into a patch of sunshine and hit the top of the stairs at a dead run, went down them three at a time and kept hoping that another fireman wasn't waiting for them at the bottom, hoping that the door was unlocked, hoping that the fireman wasn't a fast runner.

He hit the door bar with all his weight and it flew open and he was down the six steps to the ground, running as fast as he could, cutting across Harold Street with barely an eye for traffic and running across the field toward The Path. There were fields up there where he could hide, until he had to circle back home for his paper route.

At the tall Douglas firs he slowed and for the first time looked back.

No one was in pursuit, nor was Horace following. Chris lay down in the thick clumps of Oregon Grape which grew at the foot of the trees, watching the school ground as he sucked in great lungfuls of air, and wondered whether under duress Horace would fink on him.

Jockey-Boxing

They waited in their bags, the sky beyond the trees growing darker as throughout the neighborhood light after light was extinguished. Radios droned to silence. In every house fathers turned off the Molle Mystery Theater and hit the pillow with sad exhaustion. A last car passed, a slow whizz of tires.

The summer sky rolled with stars; the air was charged with the perfume of late blossoms heavy with browning scent, wisteria, pine pitch. The smells were dark as shadows, and Chris lay in his bag, unable to sleep, arms folded beneath his head, staring straight up at the stars which pulsed nearer, aware of every scent and sensation. Tires on the road, a faint radio, a cricket, the bag's odor of old sweat, fresh-cut grass, his skin.

He heard Martin say, "Okay, boah, let's go." He crawled slowly from the bag into the warm night, slipped into pants and shoes, and followed across the yard, a charge of nervous energy moving him. In the shadows beside the house, where Martin's parents slept, they moved cautiously, tennis shoes padding across the gravel. Beyond the house he felt excitement pound in his chest, becoming a giggle that he could barely hold.

Quickly they walked down the street, away from the arc light, and cut across the field until they came to pavement. Under the huge firs' shadows they surveyed the street: a new Chevvy convertible, top down. But it sat in the umbrella oflight from the house, and Martin said he saw someone on the porch. They waited, hearing the sound of their own breath.

Although it was past ten, he wasn't sleepy. In the mossy shadows the air was charged with a lazy perfume; the summer moon sailed the clear sky. He thought it was strange to be out this late, in this night world, and as he watched the dark street he felt a surge of excitement.

He had not done this kind of thing last summer—how quickly things changed, he thought. Already Martin, only a year older, was beginning to shave.

"Watchit, boah!" Martin said. Lights swept the street, a beacon's finger. The car turned the corner and halfway down the block found a driveway; they heard the car door slam, then a screen door.

They waited until the house lights went out.

He could feel the pine needles against his palms, smell their rich odor. They crouched behind the laurel hedge until the house lights went out, and then he followed Martin into the shadows beside the car, his heart bursting against ribs. Because it was summer all of the car's windows were rolled down.

He heard the click, heard Martin running his finger through the man's life: the rustle of a map, fuses, screws. He heard or thought he heard a noise from the house—the man rolling over his wife, raising himself from her to perhaps reach into the drawer for a pistol. When Martin said, "Let's go, boah," he exhaled the breath he hadn't realized he had been holding, and they were running silently into the yawning darkness of the field, toward Martin's house.

They flung themselves on the sleeping bags, gasping for breath. In the darkness Martin rattled what he had got from the jockey-box. "Got some smokes, and a damn good knife." He laid the bone-handled knife beside the crumpled pack of Luckies. Once they had got a pint of whiskey; another time a pair of binoculars.

They lay on top of their bags, debated whether to look for another car to jockey-box, and finally decided to smoke a weed. Chris took one, put it to his lips, felt the harsh tobacco. Martin had the matches out when the light flashed in the house behind them. They watched, saw a woman cross the room, disappear, then return. She reached up and began to unbutton the back of her dress.

"Sheeut." Martin crawled from his sleeping bag to the shelter of the laurel hedge which divided the two yards; Chris followed, and together they stood beneath the window, just out of the rectangle of light. The woman sleepily got the dress unbuttoned, pulled it over her head; they watched in hot amazement as she stood before them in panties and bra, her stomach rolling over the line of cloth. He watched, thinking of covers of paperback books, Sears' catalogues, comic books. She sat on the bed, her back to them, and did something with her stockings; when she stood again her hands went behind her, snaps snapped, and the bra fell away. He watched in disbelief, unable to match the real thing with his fantasies. Her hands slid panties away, falling past knees. She stood like that for a half-minute, the black mass of hair clearly visible—a fleeting vision and yet one which would haunt them for months, years—as if she knew they were there, and then she pulled the nightgown over her, stretching tight at all points, shutting off those broad expanses of skin they desired.

The light went off.

They crept back to the sleeping bags and Martin kept repeating in a sharp whisper, "Sonovabitch—gawd damn!" His head ducked inside the bag, and came out with a lit cigarette. Martin took a long drag, and passed him"the glowing coal. He was thinking of the woman; he sucked a quick puff, and blew smoke into the night. His heart quickened, the stars spun nearer.

"Gawd," Martin said, looking worldly and wise even as he expressed amazement, "I heard all women want it, but I didn't know she wants it."

He passed the cigarette back to Martin, wondering how do you know when a woman wants it? Lately he had thought a great deal about what he would do if he had the chance to kiss a girl. He thought he could do it—he had practiced on the back of his hand.

"Cheerist!" Martin said, slipping out of his Levis and into the bag. "When I get a girl, she'll do what I say. When we start going steady you can bet she'll put out." He dragged slowly on the cigarette and in the glow Chris could see the outline of his face, the serious expression; the smoke climbed the dark air, up into the trees.

Chris slipped his pants and shoes off, and crawled into the bag which was clammy with dew. He felt that Martin was full of bullshit about half the time, and yet he admired Martin's certainty, his knowledge of the world. He too would get a girl who would not laugh at his lack of experience.

"When I get a girl," Martin said, shifting closer to Chris. "Listen: all you got to do is to get her somewhere alone, see. Here's what you do: hold her hand, and swear a little. Then tell her a Johnny joke, sort of work into it. She gets hot that way—none of them can resist that stuff. Pretty soon you got your arm around her, a hand on her titty— sheeut," Martin said in a voice that carried a mature assuredness, "when I get a girl I'll have her clothes off so fast!"

What do you do then? he wanted to ask, trying to imagine himself with a girl—the faces of girls in his school flashed across his mind— sitting in the woods near his house, a bottle of his father's beer and a cigarette passed between them; as he took the butt from her lips he leaned closer, he could smell the clean innocence of her skin, their cheeks touching…

He opened his eyes, saw the fir branches weaving softly in the warm wind, felt the air brush his face, tasted the harsh tobacco on his tongue. Martin was moving around in his bag, and he said, "Colder than a witch's tit in here—can I get in yours?" Chris was surprised, because the night was warm, and so was Martin's body against his. They shifted in the small space until they lay side by side, and Chris was aware of Martin's size by the space he needed. Martin was full of bullshit, thought Chris, but he was bigger and older and he did seem to know some things. So when Martin said, "When you get a girl get her to do this," and slid his hand along Chris's leg, hip, over his stomach and down, curling it around his cock, squeezing it, Chris was surprised but remained motionless, barely breathing, listening to the branches moving overhead and thinking how he had kissed his own arm for practice, thinking how he had to learn somehow.

Merritt Clifton

Merritt Clifton is the editor/publisher of *Samisdat* magazine (Brigham, Quebec). An outspoken social and literary critic, his writings have appeared in numerous magazines and reviews.

from **24 x 12**

People had come up beside me while I puzzled. I folded my paper, tucking it in my pocket. They were three, and a blur. Girls, I thought. I shook my head, blinking my eyes to clear them. They stood maybe six feet away, talking softly and looking in my direction. They were not three, but four. I started to walk away, but they approached and I recognized them all. The first was Cynthia, a fine-haired pale blonde, a gentle sufferer in some ways, spirited in others. She used a lot of drugs. The second was Vera, her best friend and a black. She also used drugs, and I'd heard some say that she and Cynthia were prostitutes to get them, lesbians otherwise. I didn't care. I did know that both of them threw a mean rotten apple. A few months back a Mutt-and-Jeff pair named Dave Paull and Bruce Castle, who hung out with Mark Freeman, had paid me baseball cards to snipe at them with small dirt clods. I'd gone along with it to get into their gang—they weren't tough, especially, but they made their own explosives, including crude dynamite. But when I'd opened fire, Cynthia and Vera had returned it and beaten me. I took the medicine from Kearny for all of them.

The third was Bonny. I knew her only by sight, from Spanish. She sat somewhere across the room, making A's.

The fourth was Michelle, from my own neighborhood. The old lady almost didn't name my sister Michelle because she thought I didn't like her, or the name. But Michelle, with brown hair as fine as Cynthia's, and skin as pale, and as bad a reputation, had become someone special to me, though I hadn't spoken to her since we'd graduated from Oxford and come to Garfield. She'd always been sickly, and had spent her summers in Normandy with distant relatives or family friends, easy grounds for teasing. And I'd teased her badly, until one day she ambushed me after school with Joasha, then the toughest girl in the sixth grade, now at McKinley. Joasha flipped me the first time, showing Michelle how. After that she stood aside. Every time I got up Michelle threw me down, into the soft grass behind the side hedge. It was uncanny—I had everything on her. Eventually she knelt on my chest, long dress flowing around me, pounding me so gently it was like caressing. I rolled over, face down, and she kissed me atop the head. Then she and Joasha both ran. I only realized days later that they'd picked a spot for it where no one else would see, and that they'd never said a word about it to anyone else. That had been something unusual. I never teased Michelle again.

I was downright afraid of her, in a different sense from any fear I'd ever known.

They surrounded me, Cynthia closest. Taller than any, I looked down, feeling sudden hope.

"Rob, why do you hate everyone here?" Cynthia asked. She touched me. I breathed slowly, trying to keep from sobbing.

"I don't," I blurted. I knew her guy, if she had one, was Doug Fry, another doper. And Michelle's Robbie Duncan, whose band played a lot of the school dances. But I wanted to embrace her. I didn't. She backed away a little bit. Bonny fumbled for words. The two of them next spoke together.

"We'd like you to carry a petition, Rob. So that girls can wear pants to school."

I didn't know why they asked me. I didn't care. Nor did I care what the petition was for. It might have been to lynch Rob McCarver for all of me. I paused a long time before answering, only to collect my voice. These juvenile junkies, as I'd read Ann Landers calling them, looked like angels to me. Even if they did break a law with every breath. With my butch haircut and hard shell I couldn't be like them. But I knew at once these were my people. I'd be their secret soldier. Only they themselves would see me on their side. I took their petition with my right hand. Michelle extended her left. I took that too.

"Thank you, Rob. People hear you and notice you. They don't notice us."

It was a lie. I often spoke out in English and History, arguing with the teachers and sometimes winning. But nobody took my side. Except Doug Fry, it occurred to me. And these girls were usually silent and shy, when they came to class at all. Those I had in classes with me.

"You can return the petition to me in Spanish tomorrow," Bonny said. "I meant to give it to you then today, but you were busy with Debbi." I let go Michelle's hand. It almost felt as if she wanted me to keep it. I nodded, seriously, dazed as they seemingly melted away, ethereal as their own acid trips. Only the petition remained with me. And a flower where my note had been, I found, reaching into my pocket for my pen, to add my own signature. Vera's work. The others had always been in my view. But while the world still looked shitty, it felt great to be alive.

Lightheaded, I now moved toward the library.

Art Cuelho

I am a novelist and a short story writer, poet, and painter. My writing covers three locations: the Central Valley of California where I grew up on two family farms, one two miles east of Riverdale, the other out on the Westside one mile north of Five Points; the Montana prairie...especially the Indian reservations; and the road, which is concerned mostly with my travels in the American West. My longest road piece is "Road Ghost Lament," recently featured in *Forum* # 1, Pikestaff Publications, Box 127, Normal, Ill. 61761. They sent out 900 free copies; so you might be able to get one with a query. Another recent publication of mine is in *Heartland: The Central Valley*; Gerry Haslem, Ed., 110 G St., Petaluma, Ca. 94952. Besides my writing I edit *Black Jack*; it features rural writers all over America, with special focus on the West. *Pikestaff* will carry my self-review of this western publication. I also edit *Valley Grapevine*, an all Central Valley California anthology. I publish a few books every year; but do not solicit material.

Many Bends in the River

I ride this long train and wait for the caboose trailing the night to signal some kind of clue to life. Perhaps a way ofliving in the dark locomotive breath will emerge from the long haul; give me a hint of my luck with the coming dawn. I look up at the stars above the rails and wonder at my unknown fortune in some faraway space in time. I am only a momentary flash that reveals worn boot heels, bits of Denver in memory, tears of a girl in a skidrow room gone completely sour.

What is unmasked by this sudden movement; some mainline fate? Youth believes in this impossible thirst across the land. It takes to heart the chances of flight used up to be reborn again somewhere else. I am attracted to its impulse. I eagerly follow the hunt down hungry crossties, in search of something beyond abandoned station houses that I got a good glimpse of in yesterday's pouring rain.

The salvage of a dream like a hobo farewell will always be a puzzling challenge. Same as this train going by Curley's Tavern on the east end of the city's outskirts. The bright neon signs hawking at me to forget the past, red-and-yellow letters of illusion going off and on in an alcoholic fever. Yes quicksand grey of sidewalk streets familiar as the clanging of garbage can lids at three a.m. And now in my eyes across the long counter the wine and whiskey drowns the blues, but cannot hide a lover's loss of pride in a human cry.

When I hear the blear of the engine up front at another crossroads in the night, crossroads crying this train is more than a future destination, this needed journey goes beyond the earthly trek of Idaho ahead—when I see the jet black smoke rolling out and settling down in the branches of summer cottonwoods I realize it was longing that put me on board. It was a woman's hands over a hot grill that bought my ticket.

I feel the curve, the coaches leaning on their side, tons of steel taking the bend around the steep mountain. Row after row of the passenger seat backs are in an upright position and deserted in the soft rumbling, except for a solitary foot sticking up here over the top, an arm curled in sleep there, a head nested on a pillow partially visible in the aisle. My own body swings from left to right continuously, my words as I write are jarred in the shifting. I am glad because I don't desire everything neat and organized. The train wants to warm you with its rocking womb rhythm. It gives me my portrait now on the passenger window, the dark and streamlined features drawn by the passion of the headlong moment. It releases something in my face; bolted days inside a single room let go. It fulfills my need to be some other place, to always travel the deep lonesome stretches down underneath the skin where the flesh delights in being hurled, where the dream craves another tall trestle spanning the big sky.

Somehow it seems natural to begin all over once more in the darkness. Isn't the night some kind of proud brother, the new motion a curtain opened before the daily void; tearing up and up, huffing out of the iron ribcage, down down through the loam of longing, later to babysit the stars with their whistlestop harmony; later to court the moon up out of her airy haven of silver, flirting in the leaves of quaking aspen lust, the sex of each tree stark in silhouette.

I am always where the train is at the moment; going up a hill, the coach lights rolling over the ground beside the tracks, layers of lights over a mile stretch across the water, slowing down by a lake, a fire and legs, masculine forms reflected in a hobo jungle, standing up

with their hands turned downward towards the redhot coals. Slowing
almost to a standstill now. And I'm so near the stranger out there.
The complete shadow-filled silence when all this rolling mass comes
to a halt, where the wilderness is the only true civilization, where
prayer has no ghosts, where faith uses the four winds to pay homage
to God's great green plan of good.

II

Big, slow, yellow and green slopes. Haze, colossal haze high up on
the ridge; and looking down, a heavy still mass of white lumber
smoke lifting straight up and fanning out flat into layers across the
valley. Missoula written allover its face. Hereford cattle grazing in
the foothill grass and beside the train patches of barley stubble. Strips
of worked up farmland. An aluminum shed protecting bails oflast
year's hay. Roan and appaloosa horses with their colts. A skeleton
foundation of an old stone building conjuring up a dim feeling of
pioneer history. Silver grain elevators on the outskirts of the city
looming their familiar commercial hulks to the streets below.

The sun ain't even peeked over the summit yet. Why is it one
wakes up so early on a train? Is it because the night never lets you
sleep, always something unexpected to nourish around the next bend
of America—eager, brawling, a song; a rare music on rails; the brands
of the hind and the brands of people and the brands of billboards
making up some kind of standard tune. Chuck Wagon Truck Stop.
Garrett Freightlines. Gene's Double Front Payroll Checks Cashed.
"Missoula!" the conductor calls out.

A couple of railroad men cross the tracks in striped blue coveralls.
Talking, gesturing with their hands about last night's spree. A wide
grin recalling some of that strange adulterous stuff that spreads from
one barstool to another like unsatisfied lust.

New passengers are coming on. A rancher and his wife are seeing
their daughter off. She is pretty and wearing cowboy boots. I want to
know her. Brown eyes. Red hair. I went to move with that summer
dress. She waves goodbye to her parents. What excuse can I make
up to sit with her. I'll think of something. Always have. Always will.
Born for that female trouble and that alimony chill.

Not longer after the East Missoula exit I saw the sunlight on the
pine ridges, on bales of alfalfa hay, on yearlings around the saltlick,
on old mine shaft mouths and abandoned cabins, on a squirrel in
the meadow grass on its hindlegs, on strange rock hives that shield

a mountain nook, on a farmer and his shepherd dog walking out to change the sprinkler irrigation, on one colt licking another colt on the shoulder. And this wide river to greet the morning, falling down wooden bridge stretching from bank to bank, two doves flying over the water, streamers of green moss on the bottom, insects making circles on the surface, tongues offoam five feet long and a foot high, the cool mist rising on the top, mallards scooting here and there in the first light. Dawn cattail reeds in the dew's sweet coma getting all of the early warmth in the marshes, all the rich crystal reflection, all the coarse breathing of a mule deer through the nostrils. And boys in front of the vista dome window waiting for the dark of the train tunnel to giggle out their fascination in the pitch black.

Why is it that rolls of wire hung over a fence post ask to be noted; a mudhen reaching over and scratching his wing, shaking his bill; each of these scenes out of the train window. Gold Creek. First gold discovered in Montana right here. Last spike of the Northern Pacific Railroad driven here in 1883. Depot Bar and Lounge. Garrison. Deer Lodge State Prison. The towns go by quickly. Sinclair. Warm Springs and cold beer. Anaconda. Durant.

Mine gutted mountains. Mineral-colored streams. Silver Bow. Butte. Livingston.

III

It was just last night, wide awake, flat on my back in bed. This journey really began there, not being able to sleep, the very notion of returning. churning my blood. Even before my suitcase was packed with cowboy shirts, before my round trip ticket was bought, before I pulled out of the Spokane depot for my family of the Montana prairie. Surrounded by sagebrush hills, it was here their names returned. Joe and Sis Bull Tail. Rufus Biggs. Cardi Goes Ahead. Robbie Dean Plays. And the days around the cabin handed to me the choke cherry picking of late August. The cattle roundup at Jig's place in the autumn out of Lodgegrass, and farther on up into the Big Horns the Buffalo Pasture. The half gallon jugs of whiskey and wild-eyed rides through reservation coulees. Being told that some people are white on the outside and Indian on the inside. And the bucks brought down and gutted and hung on the rafters of the garage or from the limbs of a tree in the shade.

When I got off the train in Billings the first person I met was Indian Charley. He needed two bucks to get back to Hardin. It was good to hear the Crow tongue spoken again.

Going back over the rolling hills to Pryor, walking down to look at the new Sweat Lodge, going for a ride to Junior's place and seeing all the horses and the yard staked out where they are going to build their new house. Just standing out there with the Castle Rocks to the south of us, and the fresh prairie green smell. The sound of a water well being drilled, heavy and droning in the distance.

In no time I was sitting on grey and blue reef rock with ochre and silver lichen crusted on its surface. I stopped several times that afternoon in the rolling hills of Pryor. I went from draw to draw, from cedar pine to cottonwood, from rock cliff to the little finger streams that met at the bottom of the slopes and ran down green and blue to Pryor Creek. These are simple hills of beauty. They make me proud I'm a painter. The greyish sagebrush, the old grand buffalo grass beard of these ravines, and the straw-colored pockets, the hill coulee springs make me think of my palette.

Sitting on the grassy bank of a finger stream, waiting for the sprinkles to stop falling and smearing my black ink, waiting this short length of time the breeze overlaps a thousand times, all the birds, the good company of these hills, the robin's voice, doves leaving the cottonwood as I approached, the crickets in the prairie grass, rocks, sky, clouds. I am not alone here. The spirit moves along the ground and gets in the loop cactus and in the branches overhead—gets into the hair on my arms.

The little mongrel pup who follows me whines and makes a fuss. He doesn't like to stay in one spot very long. He has made himself a nest beneath a small cedar and accepts the afternoon pace from me by pulling green leaves off some red shoots coming up out of the earth.

Every man needs a place to return to when his spirit is in the mountains. Even if it's just for a day, a week, a longing need to be resatisfied.

Now the chipmunk voices his tiny bark. He came up within a few feet of me and then scampered away.

I have come six hundred miles to sit in silence under a cedar tree upon a deer bed. I will sit here beneath this single tree as long as it took me to travel the distance here by train. So I have rambled over the night trail by locomotive to sit here on the ground alone, to walk a few miles until my mouth is dry, to just wonder at what I had left behind, to what I had worked in daily. And now the sun in these hills wants to sum it up with this poem:

I walked far
into the mountains
and sat down directly
before the sun's light;
there was much space
between the silence.

I only listened;
thoughts never came.
I knew the answer would
come with the wind.
Its direction would tell
the leader of my spirit.

I smelled the perfumed sage
up over the grassy coulees.
I saw the snow on
the high blue peaks.
The reservation cedars
made me feel at home.
The single white clouds
above searched my solitude.

And then the vision
appeared in a voice:
"As many days as you sit
directly before the sun
you shall receive these gifts,
the heart of this land.
You have come naked my son,
and nakedness is your light."

IV

Outside the train heads for home, moves past an old concrete
foundation mountain bridge with a gravel roadway running out of a
grove of quaking aspen. A white milky spring coming out of brown
and sage-colored rock. A pair of magpies over the tops of pines. In
the newspaper in the man's hands in front of me one caption reads
"Sickle Death Clues Found."

It is almost night and the distance to the station easy as the rim of pink on the horizon, a white half moon, a star or two, a wide dark river enlarging the land, and giving out the evening's first goosebump chill. Soon the trees will be swallowed up by the gentle darkness. The last light on the river where fat trout make the silent circles spreading wider and wider each time they lunge for the winged insects and me, my song, my locomotive breath spread over the ramblings of youth, given up eagerly to time and flight and lust and tomorrow. Some unknown wind always to be satisfied, and a farewell note where only a handful can follow the beauty and the pain of a western night forever on the loose like the stars up above, like heaven in a gypsy's arms.

Millie Mae Wicklund

Attended Rhode Island College & graduated with a B.Ed.; studied for a year and a half at the Poetry Workshop at the University of Iowa with Mark Strand, Donald Justice, and Michael Dennis Browne.
Have published in small press magazines since 1969. My first publication was in *Trace* magazine. Magazines I appeared in: *The Florida Quarterly, Extensions, Beyond Baroque, Café Solo, DeKalb Literary Arts Journal, The Rhode Islander, Hey Lady, Rockbottom, Ghost Dance* and *The Westerly Sun.*
Have had poems in two anthologies: *I Had Been Hungry All the Years,* edited by Glenna Luschei of Solo Press and *This Is Not the Titanic* edited by C.S. Crowther of Folk Frog Press.
Books: *The Marisol Poems* by New Rivers Press and *Outlaw* by Mudborn Press.

from The Magi

...It is, as I have said, this question of what is real an ominous one and one which stops you in your tracks once in your life.

I was stopped now in my tracks. I saw now here outside the building of the insane asylum that I had been assigned to and watched for the six o'clock train to appear. And waiting for it, I went back to things in my life that I had reflected on and had talked about to my psychiatrist. What is real. I sighed, thinking of...

I. down in her pants, children playing doctor, some adults, too, like child molesters, not me, not big enough, not tom thumb either, yet, no blues, her pants, like that, a laugh, sun falling thru her eyes, the railroad tracks behind lumbering its freight cars, trains, awoee! santa fe, penn central, texas panhandle, erie coal, refrigerator cars, oil tank cars, black, brown, red, her little red dress so high in the wind, the cars rocking by, mum de mum, mum de mum, gonna be in them, yeah, whoosh, cars gone by, little red dress falls down, caboose man

swinging his lantern, back of the caboose, all the time, back of the red
(rosey is italian. is eight. like me. school is on. dinner is home.
noon. rosey, hector, me. rosey skips. hector snuggles rosey. i punch
hector. rosey punches me. hector kisses rosey. i jump on hector.
hector is a negro. hector is on the ground. rosey slaps me and runs
like hell. her legs two thin strips of white. i like white. hector's black
face is torn with white tears. i like that. nigger, i yell. white piss pot,
hector yells. i laugh. his mother told him to say that. i catch up with
rosey. she touches my face. i laugh into her hand. she smiles. we
walk along. she folds her hand. she clenches it to her side. i touch her
hand. i push my finger into the little hole at the bottom. she opens
her hand a little. i slide my finger into that. rosey laughs. she looks at
me. her black eyes fall into mine. i don't think there is any sidewalk.
or trees. or houses. I don't think there is any hector. rosey and me.
wham! the sidewalk slams into my chin. ahhhhh. red spurts out. my
head feels dizzy. i look up. rosey is shaking. rosey is in two parts.
rosey is above me and on both sides of me. brown breaks over my
head. hector is swinging his feet at me. first one foot. then the other.
i try to get up. i fall down. he steps on my hand. he dips his knee into
my mouth. more red. he pulls me. he pulls me into a tree. he pulls me
into a house. he picks me up. he pulls me up against him. his face is
everywhere. i can't see the trees. i can't see the house. but i know they
are there. i know hector is there. hector walks off with rosey. rosey's
red dress lifts a little. the wind curls it. it lifts up. i see her leg. the
wind pushes hector and rosey together. her bare leg touches hector's
corduroys.)
(spring is nice. is everywhere. squirrels pop in and out of trees
in the schoolyard. birds land on the open window sills. the sun runs
up and down the blackboard. i want to run. i want to climb a tree.
rosey and hector and me. rosey is in the front seat. hector sits under
the clock. rosey sits with her hands folded. like she's praying. hector's
knees touch the desk and lift it up. but he don't get yelled at. i'm
alone. in the back. i get yelled at all the time. i throw the blackboard
erasers out the windows. or my books. to get out. i get out. i get
yelled at. rosey peeks at me. hector peeks at me. they look at mrs.
horton. she looks like she don't wear no bra. she hangs over rosey.
they smile at each other. they smile at hector. they all glare at me.
i raise my hand and tell her my book fell out the window. the wind
comes in and she looks like she has a bra on. i laugh. she yells at me
more. hector sticks his tongue out at me. rosey sticks her tongue out
at me. i stick my tongue out back. i get yelled at again. i get up and

go out after my book. i leave the door open and the wind traps mrs. horton's blouse to her. i see rosey lifting her head up into that. i want to do something about it. i can't. i go out into the schoolyard. i get my book. bending down, a fart, a beautiful fart explodes out of me, down in my pants, a warmth, a warmth fills everything up, runs down my legs, a warmth.)

(punching, landlord and gambler dreams, musty cellar, my eye in the spider's web, whoosh, collecting it all, terror and flight, spider runs, silver threads hang down, little rosey is swinging in the tire swing, a black widow scuttling in the crust of the window in line with her feet, pierce the widow, splurt, little rosey opens her legs, kicking, pumping, ride up to heaven, rosey, ride up.)

(scars, some approved, some not. hector rips his leg open, falling down the bank behind old man willard's house. it is winter, snow is everywhere. a piece of sheet metal hidden does the job. hector is lucky. a man passing by hears him and packs snow around hector's leg. the doc says it saved hector. could have bled to death. me, I got mine running around the pole in the dirt cellar of hector's house where we used to live. my aunt put a face cloth on it. my scar on my leg is wide and ugly. hector's can't be seen. rosey hates mine.)

(school, school, school. icon rosey. hector has gypped me in a trade. i give 25 cents and a white ford for a war jeep. world war ii. i have hero dreams and ambitions. hector's ma says he got gypped for his jeep. he gets the jeep back. he keeps the 25 cents and the white ford and gives me a truck. his mother is no where around when he does this. but it is like white piss pot. the deal makes me feel this more than the words he yelled at me and i call him nigger. he calls me a name back. i'm sore. i plan to get even. i use rosey. a holiday. school is creepy. i insist that rosey go with me. i draw up an adventure. rosey is not beyond imagination. i use women the way women use men. i use hector's ma for an example. we skip school in the afternoon. we go to three blocks away. that is farther than we have ever been. houses tower over us. trees tower over us. people. we go where they're digging a hole for a gas station. it's like we're on a mountain. the man in the cab of the steam shovel towers above. he digs holes that are super. i play with cars. digging holes in the ground for them. none compare to this. rosey and i spend all our time there. we forget about time. it gets dark. we find our way back some way. everything is strange. every face is strange. but the stores. they're familiar. i get us back home that way. my mother is waiting for us. rosey's father is waiting, too. my mother is waiting in the yard under the tire swing. a cop's car is there too. i walk into the yard. wham! my mother slams me in the mouth. i don't understand. she talks funny. her words stop and go. tears fall down her face. my tears never stop. hers do. i'm scared. she is so big. her face so stern. the cop is so big. he talks to me. the words fall like rocks down a mountain on my head. worse, hector is sitting on his front steps laughing at me. then rosey's father picks me up and shakes me all over. my teeth jingle. my clothes climb up my back and up my neck. hector laughs more. rosey goes off. i go into my house with my mother. i still feel my mother's hand. i remember standing there smiling up at her. i want to tell her what i've seen. wham! the way the slap came was like having to give the jeep back. i sit up in my bedroom with the street lights on and watch hector sitting on his front steps playing with the jeep. rosey sits with him. hector's mother comes to the door and smiles at him. i hear my mother down in the kitchen. i feel my face pull together. i have been terribly put down this week. i think hector's ma is better than mine. she stuck by him. got him the jeep. lights. rosey. everything.)

(summer and i think of long days with rosey. but there are not going to be any long days. rosey is moving. they are to leave tonight. i cannot eat my supper. i want to go and see rosey off. my mother scolds me. finally she lets me out. i stand in front of the restaurant on the hill. i feel like i'm going to fall down the hill. I can't keep my balance. rosey comes out and smiles at me. she is laughing and dancing around. the hill doesn't bother her. hector is there too. all the suitcases are packed. hector kisses rosey. she kisses me. i don't like sharing. i wish she had just kissed me. or hector. she sits in the back seat, peering out the window waving goodbye. they don't even stop at the red light. i see rosey waving for a long time. i walk down the hill still tottering on my feet. i sit down in front of the fish market. the smell of fish is awful. i feel sick to my stomach. hector is at the top of the hill. i'm sitting at the bottom. all of a sudden vomit erupts out of me. a train goes by. the whole hill shakes. hector comes down and stands over me. the fish smell gets to him. he wrinkles up his nose. he kicks at the front of my shoe. ah, he says, and ambles off. he holds his stomach. i run after hector and bump his elbow with my elbow. he puts his arm around my shoulder. we walk down the street laughing. the next day we take our bicycles to the top of the hill and ride like hell down it and slam on our brakes. the smell of black scorched rubber mixes with the smell of the fish market. the man comes out and chases us away. we ride up the hill to the restaurant and sit on the steps. we peer inside. hector gets up and on his bike and rides

silently off. i follow him. we get a red light and ride right thru it. we
end up at the excavation hole that i took rosey to. only this time it is
a completed gas station. hector fills his back tire with air and rubs
at the burns on the tire. we look at the gas station for a long time
and finally hector mumbles, it was better the other way, and we ride
off, leaving the smell of gas for the smell of fish. both remind me of
rosey. they weren't so bad when rosey was here. at the corner of the
fish market near the red light hector tells me he is moving in a week. i
lose control of my bike and plow into the side of a white ford. hector
looks at me. i look at hector. the hill towers above us. a train goes by.
the smell of the fish and the gasolene meet together under the red
light. summer has just begun.)

(rain falls down. under the pole where i cut hector and rosey
off one day causing rosey to fall off hector's bike, a puddle collects,
little sticks bumping up against each other in water. i go out and
watch them loading suitcases. hector says they are going to detroit.
automobiles are made there, he says, and hands me the jeep and
smirks. all the suitcases are packed. hector gets in the back seat. he
grins thru the glass. the rain is pouring down my neck and my clothes
are getting limp and uncomfortable around me. the jeep in my pants
pocket rubs against my leg. hector sticks his hand out the window
and yells, so long, teddy, in a rough boyish voice that is affectionate. i
run up and hold his hand. then he is gone. i go over and kick thru the
puddle. all the little sticks are separated.)

caboose, little rosey runs thru the field, running thru the field,
running thru the wild buttercups and the four leaf clovers, running
under and in and out of the sun, her little red dress kicking, kicking
up into the air, her little white pants looking up, looking up all the
way to heaven.

II.   to stomach america, you have to put up with pants, sun,
rain, wind in trees that you can't see the tops of and whispers in
corridors or houses or mouths: the lips of women always move in
consequences that men mostly ever after vagrant explore and exploit
in larger things and ways than a pair of legs in silken cloth or bare
arms near a guitar or a vase of flowers as if the world were commerce
or business but derelict for months I cannot recall a venture that
stopped anyone or anything like a woman stopping a child in puberty
or a man in the act of love and childlike, Rimbaldian or Lawrentian,
or even as a blue butterfly, after memory, in and about it, what
nuance exists, IS was cliché, her mouth removing the larger risk,

calculation, invention, and spirit is maybe the movement of her body, liquid or dry, behind words whose shadow is down an alley where the clown who still performing evokes laughter from a man who said and did escape crazy sorrow to sorrow more crazily in an honest vomit or a dazzling confession while railroad wood flames a fire that a city's torment drove to metaphysics that intellectuals raid or eulogize while the poet, the man with a price on his morality, lover, public, whose words the bum drinks from the bottle that a de leon or catullus scrapped until the sculpture arose out of the nothingness of venture: the poet topping agony, I, I, I,

(I am memory at most. at most all is there. so a small boy. and lonesome is as lonesome does. I'll be this. I'll be that. acting ritual and, rites. celebrate. protest. eulogize. picking up petulance and weakness along the way.)…

the journal

Geoffrey Cook
Holly Anderson
David Ossman

Geoffrey Cook

Education: Shaker Heights High School, Kenyon College, A.B.
(Majors: Classical languages & English). I also spent a summer
at the Aspen Writers' Workshop under a scholarship.
Job background: During my summers between semesters, I
worked for the City of Shaker Heights (a suburb of Cleveland,
Ohio) Recreation Program. I conducted games, taught
crafts, & eventually worked into a supervisory capacity over
programs for junior and senior high school students. After
college I worked at the Cleveland Museum of Art in an intern
program. One of my duties was speaking to high school
groups & conducting them about the Museum. For two years,
I was traveling & studying in Asia. For four years, I worked
for the Museum Society of the Fine Arts Museums of San
Francisco both in the M.H. DeYoung Memorial Museum & the
California Palace of the Legion of Honor. I've also conducted
poetry workshops at Folsom Prison on a volunteer basis.
Last spring I was employed by the Adult Division of the San
Mateo County Schools teaching creative writing. I hold a valid
teaching credential in the State of California.
Publications: *Tolle Lege* (Moonbird Publications, UK, 1974);
*Love & Hate: Translations from the Carmina of Gaius Valerius
Catullus* (Outrigger Publishers, New Zealand, 1975); *Selections
from the Miscellanea of Venantius Fortunatus* (Cherry Valley
Editions); *THE: Texts and Explanations* (Laughing Bear Press).

The United States of America A Travel Sketch
after Bassho

"To add to their difficulties, the time came when
the guides admitted that they no longer knew
the way; all the marks, they declared, had been
obliterated by the blown and drifting sands."
Arrian: *Anabasis of Alexander* VI:26

Time…jangled…travelling many international flights. Boarded plane in Tokyo, December 28th/12 noon. It's 10 PM, December 27th. Honolulu is numberless lights. Landing rough/raining:

U.S.A.
Honolulu lights
    from dark Pacific
plane buffets through turbulence
Drizzling on ground.

Customs pleasant. Don't search. Never been searched by American customs.

I say good-bye. Was to stay in Hawaii. Plans changed. I'm sad & unhappy. Told to go to Florida. No desire to re-enter States—much more the Mainland. Drizzle is downpour.

"Continuation of JAL Flight 006 to San Francisco loading at Gate 8."

Growling jets
(Surf on beach)
To be with you
    in morning
        when ocean breeze
            ruffles your hair.

Lights outline shape of Diamond Head. Feel like crying. Thoughts go to conversation with young soldier flying between Chicago & Cleveland, a year before—whose brother had just been killed in the War…

…Captain announces rough journey to California. Apprehensive. Thoughts wander to incidents while still in Ohio…11-1/2 months before, I was held captive by 15 Black Panthers / spat upon / called bourgeoise poet / my friend & associate, Franklin Osinski beaten up twice / face bloodied. Nine months ago, multi-media show I produced raided by police / claiming we were smoking marijuana. Friends have been thrown in jail—trumpt-up charges; others fled country—some still fleeing—some dead…murder / suicide. Big Northern cities no longer fit for meditative &/or creative life. Mr. & Mrs. America, this is true! It is spreading:

America
I have searched on many days
in many different places
the highways of central Ohio
the hills of San Francisco
the valleys of Pittsburgh
the towns of South Dakota
the mountains of Colorado
the deserts of Nevada
The hounding never stops
the hunters are clever
fear is always there
gnawing like a cancer through my intestines.

Dawn over Pacific. Santa Cruz Mountains! & south Bay.
Approach takes us over Bay fills. Ecology of the West Coast is
delicate. Fills have raised annual mean temperature by 2 degrees.
Would take only small earthquake in right place to change Japanese
Current & San Francisco would have New York winters. Plane is
taxiing to terminal…

It is a balmy day. A friend meets me, & takes me into the City.
I'm glad to see a friend. He wants to know about India. What's
there to tell? (I tell him something, though). I'm left-off at the Yoga
Center on Sacramento Street. I spend a frantic hour finding a place to
stay. Joel Deutsch, poet invites me over for the day. I walk to Geary
Avenue; then up to Third Avenue. Sky is clear & sun is warm—
remarkable for the 28th of December. San Francisco is magical—it
always is / City of emerald & gold:

San Francisco
1.

My Lady
This City of Dreams
who has embraced me
into her psychedelic slumber
of red
gold
purple
& orange

who has encumbered me
               with her Minor key rhythms
                              of blues
                              soul
                              jazz
                              & rock

Neon mistress
               returning to you
                              is like receiving an estranged lover
                              who has come
                                             to renounce her infidelities
                                             to lie with me
               slumbering in this dream
                              my dream
                              the Whore of the Age
                              the Whore of a Thousand Years

Dream me your pimp
               Lady
               for where can I go
                              that your jasmined tongue
                                             won't whisper
                                                            tunes of June nights
                                             on upland summer roads

I'm so weary
       so world weary

And the Lord said: "I will save this City
                              if I can find one righteous man"
But the Angel replied:
       "Only I have survived alive"

2.
Interlude

Black children playing in the Panhandle
afternoon traffic trudging Fell Street
the smell of grass after rain...

City, you've always struck a Minor key
>your Victorian townhouses painted with psychedelic hues
>& the flesh tones of Columbus-Broadway...

3.

So come to me now
>lie with me now
>>neon, mountains, & sea
Fade into me
>>the cold ocean at my feet
>>(the edge of this world!)
>>this warm day...

Joel & I rap. I'm nervous from travelling. I talk too much. Joel has shaved his beard—too many girls on Telly thought he was Allen Ginsberg. (What a *karma* to have on your face!) He's going to Sacramento to see Doug Blazek & D.T. Wagner; he invites me.

Trip to Sacramento—70 miles on Interstate 80. Over Coastal Mountains; smog lifts. Chilly day in Valley—in summer flatter &: hotter than Kansas. D.Y. & Doug live in a straight neighborhood. Haven't seen D.Y. since one of levy's Gate readings in Cleveland, 1965. He's grown long hair & a beard—a fine adaptation to California. We speak of old friends. I'm a little manic from travelling. I talk & talk. Carl Woideck arrives from Berkeley. He invites me to stay at his place. (I have no place to crash); I accept. Joel & I go—to see Doug Blazek, legendary Underground poet. Remember my first meeting with Doug 1-1/2 years before. Looking for the Willie (hidden in San Francisco). At the corner of Haight & Masonic / wonderous corner of freaks & dealers. Now Spades & speed-freaks. Walk up hill almost to Fredrick Street. Ring Doug's bell. Expect to see long-haired head. Clean-cut slightly plump young man says:
"Yes."
"Does Doug Blazek live here?"
"That's me."
Polish boy from Chicago. True proletariat poet like Eric Hoffer is a proletariat philosopher. Doug raised in working class / worked in factory / understands father's world / understands hip / lives between two—weakness & strength. Has discipline (like D.Y.) to

bring goals through. Riff for several hours. Crash on couch—first sleep for three days. .

Wake next morning. Joel & wife still there. Say good-bye to Blazek's. Leave for City. California. California, the Golden—the promised land of the promised land. No, I did not miss Ohio, nor Nevada, nor New York, nor Florida. I missed California. California, every nut / weirdo / Communist/ Fascist/ Hippie/ Surfer / Faggot/ red-neck freak must be here. I can see the Bay; smog quickly covers view. Vallejo, Richmond, El Cerrito, Berkeley, Oakland—the Bay Bridge.

I gather my things together. Trying to change dollar for the Muni: "Get out of here you fuckin' freak!"

Berkeley. Broke / Hungry. Showing-up at dinner sometimes fills my belly. Sick. Go to free clinic. Waiting 6 hours. Talking to nice little Hippie chicks. All had clap. What a drag! Doctor tells me to go to emergency at Kaiser Hospital in Oakland. Gives me directions to hitch. I find ride. Wait four hours. Two people die—one Spade from police bullet. Screaming relatives. Another brought on stretcher. Throat hemorrhaging from cancer. Old mother holding his head blood on her lap. He dies. She just sits:

Oakland Emergency Room

God, if you could only scream
        the cancer eating your throat
gagging & coughing in the next room
gurgling for me, My Baby
& the ambulance
thinking it was I
        an old lady
                dying of her heart
      not hearing your gasping screams
            like 40 years ago...

you were so helpless
        in your crib
Moma would caress you
Moma is still caressing you
           speeding / through the city...

"Death, where is Thy sting?"
just this exhaustive loneliness
                waiting / for the cab...

Finally talk to Doctor. Gives me a shot. Says I'm suffering from
vitamin shortage—had dysentery in Nepal.
     Noise! Noise! There is no silence. Noise! Noise! on the radio:

                "Down by the river
                I shot my baby."

Psychedelic music. Loud music! Can't meditate. Try to keep
my forces together. Generation on speed. Running down to Avenue
/ find something to do! Do! Do! Do! Done! Did! Action! Speed!
Revolution! Fill senses...overfill with loud music / drugs / sex...Got
no time to stop! ...think...

        California rain
        cold, drizzly rain
            winter rain
                for days
                    soaking
                    strange city
                        & cold
                            wandering from pad to pad
                                    trying to work
        Loud psychedelic music
        "Gotta move
                move
                run
                run to Avenue
                get more dope
                        dope
        We're outta dope
                & speed."
        Can't see mountains of Marin
        Smog too heavy.

Spend New Year's Eve on move. Into City. Stop at house once
stayed at on Downey Street. Had turned into a slum. Cross City to
rich Hippie party. Bird-dogged someone's Old Lady. Back in Berkeley.

5 AM. Then, to Mount Tamalpais in Marin:

> New Year's sun emerging from America
> Drizzle over Bay
> (Dark still conceals Pacific)
> City's lights fade.

Received money. Was eating. Felt better. Found place where I sometimes could meditate. Walked streets alot. Poem I wrote similar time 2112 years previously:

Haight Street Blues

> San Francisco, City of dreams
> > > acid visions
> of Delilahs
> > hugging long-haired Samsons.
> Birds are gliding in stormy sky
> as clouds part to sun
> & I feel the flow
> > > of life
> as I once felt
> > > cold waters of northern Appalachian streams
> flow past
> > my body
> > long ago.

Found ride to Miami on U.C. ride board. Had week to wait.

Went with pusher-friend to Black dude's store. Friend wanted to sell owner dope. Name AUM. "I am AUM sacred word of the Vedas, sound in silence; heroism in men." Krishna to Arjuna, Bhagavad Gita 7:8. This AUM looking for key—wild hair/bright clothes. Naked chest. Had white chick-pale. Sitting in hammock seductively staring. Could see cunt & boobs through thin nightgown. Early Dylan on stereo. Dealer & AUM...pot & opium. AUM started preaching from Upanishads. Acid-filled eyes glaring into mine. Telling me how he met God, & what the Dude said to him. One...Two...Three hours. Key is unwrapped. Too many twigs. He neatly re-wraps it without losing a word. Takes another 1-1/2 hour to split

Collage
to the Pop Culture

Mannequin dolls
skin so white
(coffin pale)
dressed in black
walking by department store window

      "I'm going downtown
      'cause I need a fix,"
            Car radio blares
            & the women come & go
                    black blouse
                    white-fringy lace
                    bell-bottom pants
          The Angel of Death carries a whip!

      "I don't know
      just where I'm going
      but I'm going to try
      for the kingdom
      if I can
      because it makes me feel like I'm a man
      when I put a spike into my vein..."

Neon paradise
motorcycle formations
beer & boobs
erotic dreams for sale
Shiva's strength being sucked
          from his groin

      "Hey, Man, do you need some speed?"
          The Revolution has come!
         A rapid transit whisks
            faster ... faster
               thru the City

      "Where's it happening?"
      "What's happening?"

"I don't know
but I've got to go
& find it!"

. . . .

"Man, this can't be it!"
"Dig it!"

The juke box rattles
people pound on the counter
           "Don't you want somebody to love?
           Don't you need somebody to love?
           Wouldn't you love somebody to love?
           You'd better find somebody to love!"

                    Sweet smell
              "Pass the dope!"
                    The dawn
                    Clutch onto it!

                         Her?

the women
the woman
      freaky Delilah
           girl of my dreams
cut off all my hair
now I'm too weak to ball
besides I have the clap
? lately I've noticed my eyes yellow
Yes
           "Happiness is a warm gun."

                    Rain
                    Sunday morning
                    coming down
                    birds are chirping...

My ride arrives at 9:30 AM Sunday, January 11 tho Down
University Avenue, I leave with regret...We hit the Freeway at
University Avenue. Take 1-580 in Oakland; over Coastal Mountains;
through Castro Valley; to Sacramento Valley; hit Interstate 5; ends

at California 152; follow east...see snow of Sierras through fog.
(Remember five months in Reno & Virginia City last summer:

> From Virginia Mountains
> > Truckee Meadows
> > Washoe Valley & Lake
> > Snow-covered Sierras
> > Haze over Reno
> On Valley floor
> > > mountain-awed
> > > cattle ranches
> > > cars passing
> > > sage & dust
> In Reno
> > no haze
> > neon
> > casino's & stores
> > few drunk cowboys.)

Hit U. S. 99...south through Madera / Fresno / Bakersfield.
People with rich hippie & his old lady. Travelling straight, but
sprouting all cliches...going to Florida to buy boat. Feels can live off
interest of dead Daddy's money. Chick half digging it. Is Libra. We
get along fine...Try to meditate...Cat can't keep quiet...try to keep
my energies...

Child

"...And the Dragon stood before the woman who
was about to bear a child, that he might devour
her child when she brought it forth..."
Revelations 12:4

Child of the day
child of the night
I have seen you in the day
> in the night
> > through bright neon lights
> > > colors
> > throbbing music
> > > incense

                    perfumes
              bare-breasted girls
                    dancing.

Child, I have seen you cry
        the serpent rise
                his teeth gnawing your eyes.

It is dusk when we approach the San Bernardino Mountains. We enter the clouds:

                    Mountains into clouds
                    Light fades into mist
                    Coming down
                        it is night

And it is L.A. L.A.! Whorehouse of the Mind…labyrinth of freeways…land of total insanity. I feel a poem I wrote several months before:

                    L.A. International Airport

              Thick smog
              Plane held
              I sit with drink
                    watching Mexican kids
                            People from Tokyo & London at customs
              Plane called
              . . . .
              The Los Angeles of the Mind / racing.

Watching competition on freeway, Golden State Freeway to San Bernardino Freeway, I-10—at the other end Tallahassee & Jacksonville only a continent away. Wheels spin past Pomona / Ontario…stop at San Bernardino truck rest. Ted insists only way to make friends is to play 3 Johnny Cash discs on the box. Puts in his quarter:

                    "I shot a man in Reno
                    just to see him die."

Redlands...Palm Springs...Indio, the desert; we turn south on California 86...past Salton Sea...over the Mojave to Brawley...El Centro, Imperial Valley; turn onto U.S.-California 80—intermittingly Interstate 9—crossing Colorado River Delta...bridge across the Colorado, new time zone, Arizona, Yuma. Ted's woman born in Yuma left when she was 6 weeks...driving to Gila Bend...hit Tucson before dawn...light on desert...surreal...weird mountains...we stop at small town near Tombstone for breakfast...Head for nearby campground...take out sleeping bags to crash...couldn't sleep... thought of the women I've left

Maya

1

She comes at night
        when freezing rain pelts window
        & people scuffle past house
She tip-toes
& silently slips her negligee to the floor
        nuzzling under covers
Her cold toes run my warm legs
I awake...

2

My old body is on display
All my children say it's a pity
They must leave at 11.
If only she would sneak into my coffin tonight
& lie with me
      take my stiff hand over her young body
      let me feel her soft breasts
         firm thighs...

I arise & do Hatha Yoga & meditate. I notice a thin layer of snow on mountains:

      Arising to morning
      looking inward
      I see snow on mountains.

I talk to Shirley who has wakened. Ted rises. We roll our bags. East towards New Mexico...afternoon:

> Cloudless
> mid-day desert sun
> Brown-baked land
> few sage brush
> A sudden breeze!...
> (Ominous sky
> hitting wind
> falling snow)
> It is winter at home

Into New Mexico. Stop to have tires checked. Bought two new tires before we realized that Cracker service attendant had suckered us. Past southern New Mexican towns on 1-10. Denning...others... desert...desert bum:

> Cold breeze
> Highway
> Old man walks shoulder.
> Passing cars
> Hands numb
> legs tire...

Discover Ted is carrying .38. Paranoid of Southern cops...Try to talk him into sending it ahead...is manic...paranoid...Las Cruces... EI Paso & Texas, central time zone. Have to stop at immigration roadblock, looking for Mexican wetbacks in Texas desert...Ted smart mouths officer...the Man wants to see our trunk (that's where Ted has the gun)...I talk to him...lets us go...dusk, again...stop at small Texas town for a meal. Mexican meal—best I've had in months... travelling for hours over Texas desert...about midnight stop at truck rest...bad vibes...Ted insists on going in...notice local sheriff...Ted sees hip hitchhiker—heading West from New York...stuck here...Ted talks loudly of drugs & politics...can hear rednecks at next table... hate hard to explain; asininity is equally as hard...finally get him away...don't think hitch-hiker made it, tough...Through the desert for hours...began to hallucinate—saw mountains; felt space inside car expanding; road seemed circular. Ted took over. I slept for first time since California. Dreamed of Yogaswami, deceased great guru of northern Ceylon, guru of my guru:

> An august crowd
> > to see the great Yogaswami
> I wander among people
> > as guru changes into bird
> > > parrot
> > > > with green
> > > > > purple
> > > > > > red. markings
> > > flies through assemblage
> I am consumed .with devotion
> > on my knees
> bird lights on my head
> > pulling hair with talons.

It is dawn again. We throw our bags open in a roadside park…
………………………Few hours later notice cold…journey resumes.
Decide to by-pass San Antonio & head up towards Austin. Stop at
small restaurant, young waitress from Natchez: "I like Texas just
fine: less Nigras & more Mexicans"…in the car I think……Wheels
crossing Texas…to Houston…we stop for an early dinner in
Houston…Beaumont…Louisiana, deep South…darkness, again…
Lake Charles, steel mills & industrial smut…cross the Mississippi
at Baton Rouge. Suggest we stop. Ted wants to make it through
Mississippi & Alabama. I say if you're able to drive. He's worn at the
Louisiana- Mississippi border. We stop at rest station next to bayou
with mourning trees…trashed, but couldn't sleep—saw visions—
demons / glaring / snorting like once at Pondicherry:

> Vine-grieving cypresses from bayou
> Green & red demons applaud night
> Breeze awakens.

Wake Ted. Tell him to move. Something wrong. Will do driving.
He's superstitious—I'm intuitive / obeys me…into Mississippi—I feel
blackness:

> "Mississippi find another country to belong to"

Ted is bitching. Has headache. Forgets fear. Through Gulfport…

demands car stop at Biloxi on a side street. I argue—I Ching warned me against legal entanglements. Twice police patrols shine lights on us, but don't accost. Sun rises. Head out. See devastation of Hurricane Caroline. Rubble still on streets...boats...gutted buildings...4 months after. Sleep to Mobile. Argument in Mobile. Ted wants to go to northern Florida. Had given him money for Miami. Convinced him to go to South Florida. Cross Mobile Bay at dawn & sleep in Alabama campground. We wake round noon...cross into Florida panhandle...past Pensacola...takes most of day to reach Tallahassee. We eat dinner...dark when we leave 1-10 for 1-75. Radio plays Simon & Garlunkel tune:

> "And they've all come
> to look for America"

*

America I've searched for You on many different days & in many different ways. You're becoming more elusive—the America I believe exists is hiding...about to go into exile...your children no longer love You...You have given them television & called it real— "reality is only the hallucinations we have in common" & I'm sick of hallucinating the Ed Sullivan Show; the Vietnam War on the Huntley-Brinkley Report. I'm an artist & no one can guarantee my physical safety to create. I don't want to destroy You, nor own You, I only want the right to work & meditate & to create. America, I have searched & searched & searched. And, America, I found You—on a road in South India:

> Humid still
> Cawing crows
> Banyan & mango trees
>
> 5 O'Clock
> Two old Tamil men hobble road
> Weather-beaten Anglican church
> Smell of manure from sugar cane fields
> 30 crumbling graves
>   covered with myriad vines
> feast of long Brahmin cow.

Rain pours hard throughout southern Florida. Dawn in Miami & rain & cars searching for their day. Crossing Rickenbacker Causeway over Biscayne Bay to Key Biscayne. In land of palms, again…Passing President Nixon's house: "Restricted"; guards…I find my parents' house…3-3⁄4 days passed from California…not bad time.

December 28, 1969—January 15, 1970

Holly Anderson

Holly Anderson was born in Minnesota on the Iron Range. By age 9 she had been baptized a Lutheran and later a Catholic. She dropped out of a Minneapolis art school in 1974 and since then has worked that series of jobs all people with no marketable skills work.

Journal Entries

BUT IT IS DEATH FOR MEN TO SPY ON WOMEN'S MYSTERIES

This book gets out of hands again. 2 months passed and I'm sitting in some chair reading notice of woman who'll teach a journal workshop and hey, I can do it again. High and Slow Thinking now—with cold fingers on a Dog's Paw Hand. rocking rocking with empty plates int he head. do the unfocus. Hear the diesel sounds with my nap up. I like the sounds that reach and touch my back. so this is partly about September that comes Cold now Mornings. With rises, the sun narrow bar   brilliant bar of some incredible neon stuff. An Edge. I like it speeking me up. It speeds me up. The cold does it. The herb does it. The fast does. And the love does it. Makes Energy. Knits It Full Of Lights And Second-Long Trances.

next day and where I sit chickens walk close with large muddied claws. beadbright stupid eyes after my boney feet and on yet another stove some sauce cooks. Full of overripe tomatoes and celery and Big Onion. Christ but all the men and all their stoves and all the sauce that's been cooked by me. in Michigan at the orchard on that low wood stove
cooking it so slow jamming it with mushrooms, with curiosity cos my Sister was coming in. And drinking far too much Homemade Beer. Staying up with that sort of drunk rocking on the porch watching the Heat Lightning break because I was fucked up in that

place where there is no sleep. Deciding then, and how many times prior, that the solitary night was the best for me. When there's no one to warm you or talk dreams aloud to a bed isn't such a marvelous thing. Instead is place to pile books and cups and empty glasses and socks. Eat messy breakfasts in and not bother about jam on the sheets. Do I want it that way? For all the time? In recollection those months Loom Positive, Radiate a Strength but oh I do remember waking up alone & wanting someone to toast bread for. And truth seems to be when I'm not steady with a man I'm in a bar or a theatre looking for him. Got my lamps lit, got my brilliant mantle on for the search. Someday someday a man that knows when to leave me to my own, when to be there and that union will be goddamn all Energy and Accomplishment.

§

on a lake. on one of the First Fine Days of May. 2 woodpeckers redheads nearly as tall as me. and in a low spot where I piss among ferns, curling brown this dry spring, large remnants from the Giant Insect Wars. and the sun goes down and all the beer is in me. through woods I make enormous noise with shoes and hands Drunk but Reverent. tomorrow I'll be busy with ticks. in the meantime:
> the bang of the boat. aluminum.
> chain saws heard across water.
> all the birds are here.
> voices under a window waiting for wood ducks to nest.
> mosquitoes or flies in the hair.
> brown curled-fur dog.
> beers opened with pocketknife.

Like the most pointed Light like the single electric light of a small
house on a narrow mooned black prairie   as fast as flicking it on
and the Light Shooting out straight and rapid to Touch the
Dark   to Touch your Mouth in the dark I would cross the
Dakotas cross the Wyomings cross myself with the Woman Musk
and the Magic   cross myself with an Angel   cross myself
with a strong fast horse   cross myself with half your Blood
and take from you and lay to rest in me all your sorrows   cross
myself with Cleopatra and Hippolyta and Lady Brett Ashley. Christ,
baby, if I knew the Incantation that could keep me near
you   keep us in those enchanted tinted places tinted lips tinted
tits tinted touch of your finger to any any part of me if I knew the
Song to Sing and you knew to hear it I swear you would not be
unhappy with my tune.

§

6/10   Not the clacking, lit up sort that causes books to be finished
at first light or fabricates tranced, perfect letters from air, wool,
shadows but the Deadening Insomnia. That kind, controlled all the
nights this past week. roll and hunch and bitch in the black. up from
that cross bed at nine or ten a.m. dulled and aching. aware in the
morning of what I need for a calm, full sleep and that knowledge
brings a bent and funny smile. Goddamn this salty, Insistent Body
that carries me. she Rave. she always Ravenous. she always In Need.
the little Spirit she says she can do without the good dinner and the
man body in the dark and the icy beer afterwards or the Heavenly
French Bottle but the Body says "Impossible!" "Essential." And the
Skin and the Hair and the Hunger always win out over the Holy Air
in the candled cave.
     spirit dream: aesthete
     body dream: harlot

§

Last nt. on that pitch black road I told them how the cousins used to catch fireflies and smash them and we'd Smear Their Light On Our Faces. And dance glowing on Burntside or Signe's River.

This late summer I see the first Northern Lights; Japanese Paintings   Color Washes   Projector Light Lantern Light   Message Light. That unknown magic passage of spirits. Across Black Curve   Black Arch   Black Guardian of Heavenly Voodoo.

§

12. 23. This one the final Christmas at eltern's. It's not simple here or joyful enough. Time now for my own celebrations. Hear too many ankle bells dream Heat Snakes Emerald and Blood Feathers. Hear too many drums to continue the awkward snow dances. A finality sits in my belly. The best Burgundy sits in my belly. I skate slow to a drunk and listen to a Brazilian sing Bone Loose & Sweet. And play Gato then. Man I've been the most intimate with.

This nt. a thick twist of Longing. On the heat I pour alcohol to desensitize the ache. Dull the edge that hungers for fur fur the arch and moan oh Christ, but I'm Wasting. Such lovely, loving pieces untouched. I walked wide open all this yr. Receiver tuned to such a fine point that light hurt and clothing chafed. And so few came. Eyes Eyes Voices but not often enough the Talking Hands Latin Tongues or Cocks to Break the Dreams Bend the Bed Soil the Immaculate Sheets.

Bottle isn't tall enough. I'm waxing these months. I am. Into Woman I Can Be: Strong and Rabid & Yielding and Full of Peace. Where's the man that can hold me right? Be my Brother be my Baby be my Lover Without End Amen

§

§

This is Chinese Year of the Horse and this is Hoarse White Woman Hollering in the dark in her hand in her hole, small place of such pleasures. but maybe this moan comes to habit. yes is habit. And the days and the dark aren't divided into deprivations and desires because I know This Peace is true. this peace this minute rests light in brittle beautiful hands and I swear to God a birthday was never as fine. as fine as finding that chugging singing glowing reed that runs strong, straight through the whole girl system.

§

David Ossman

I began keeping a more-or-less daily journal, just after moving
to Santa Barbara. Earlier, I kept diaries or journals on trips
or other special occasions (like "Portrait Painiting"). I've also
used journals indirectly—to write "finished" poetry—and
directly, as in my book *The Crescent Journals* where the poems
and fragments make up a temporal record. Since 1970, readings
from the *I Ching* have formed a continuous log of emotional
change, co-existing with post-facto recollection.

Portrait Painting

FIRST SITTING

Much time spent arranging the pose, positioning two benches on
top of which, a chair. M has decided to use a small board and it has
been prepared with a smooth coat of white. It will be an intimate
pose, a bust, the lights are arranged and I take off my glasses, sitting
in the chair, giving M a more than three-quarters pose. (He will have
nose trouble, but neither of us suspect it now.) I am very cheerful, it
is a beautiful day, the studio is warm. My pose is not uncomfortable,
but my shoulder is giving me trouble, and I stare off at the corner of
the room, seeing the paint spatters on the wall in a blur. The lights
are not troublesome. M draws in the basic pose on the white board
in brownish paint. I cannot see what he is doing. We sit and paint
for a half-hour or so. Talking occasionally. We are both cheerful. It
is not going well and we take a break. M has placed the image in an
awkward opsition, I think. It is too small and off-center, requiring
something to be done about the background. It is a recognizable
likeness, but not me.

We spend another three or four hours at it, in about half-hour
sittings. It gets dark outside, which changes the light. I smoke a good
deal, and we talk happily about a lot of things. We break for dinner.
It is not going well. M talks to himself, looks at the ptg in the mirror,

has much trouble with the clothing, which he does not like. He also has trouble with the nose, particularly. I do not like my hair. He takes a break to the background and tries to suggest a landscape. "What would you like?" "The coast." He does not paint the coast. It does not go well. We have a good dinner and go back out about 8:30 or so. Look at the ptg. I look very young, somewhat puffy. M paints a little more and says that we obviously can't do it in one sitting. Neither of us are satisfied and the light has changed completely. I go home.

§

SECOND SITTING

M has dropped a blue blanket from a rafter in back of the chair to close off the area. It is a very windy day. Where is the ptg? M has painted it over and sets up the board with a uniform earth/brown color (burnt umber, mixed with grey, he says). We decide to cover the big window, because of the light problems, and the wind blows against the canvases he sets up against it. We choose another pose, so I am now looking at the easel supports, and the nose is easier to paint. On the easel support are two paint spots which I think look like Hebrew letters. They are about all I have to look at, unless I angle my eyes over to try and see the ptg. This is possible when M swings the easel around my way.

I am comfortable, feel good except for the shoulder, take off my glasses and look at the Hebrew letters. The radio/phono is in the studio and we listen to Bach, Joan Sutherland, and chamber music by Mozart, Schubert and Schoenberg. Very pleasant and not much talking.

M works rapidly, rubbing the brown paint away to show the white underneath and sculpts my portrait, hardly adding any paint from the brush, but wipes and drybrushes it with a two-inch brush to smooth out the image. I take a break and look at it. It is going very well. Looks like me, the parts of the face seem better oriented. The image takes up more of the board than before. M works very hard on getting the features. Brushes in some background paint, tries several ideas with clothing.

I am wearing a bulky cardigan as for the first sitting, but it does not work out. Eventually I get a sort of turtleneck ruff in red. Much time spent on the clothing and the background color and M is frustrated. The image looks great. We joke about it: "Westward the course of Empire," as I look like an Upholder of the British Raj staring off over the Khyber Pass. But it does look like me; in a farsighted sort of way, the image is clearly myself. We started about noon. The wind is very strong. We break for lunch.

I tell M that he should stop worrying about the background and the clothes because he can paint them without me there, and that he should go back to the face. The face looks great, just the rubbed brown over white, with a few brush strokes around the eyes and some modeling on the cheeks. I expect him to start glazing, tho I'm not sure just what glazing is. It goes wrong. He mixes flesh-tone paint and starts adding to the surface. We decide that it's mixing two techniques: building up on the surface and sculpting away into the surface. Very quickly I have a mask of pinkish paint which obscures all the fine modeling. It is a layer of makeup. All wrong. M is very unhappy. Tries to wipe some of it away and to model other parts of it. Immediately the face is unlike mine as to proportion and placement of features. The British Raj thing is gone, which doesn't bother me especially, because it was a little corny, altho I do have that farsighted look which comes from nearsightedness, and I do have that sort of nose-in-the-air thing, which we used in 1957 to make the first portrait of me as an Elizabethan fop. But all of this is gone. He is sweating over it. I say, "I didn't mean for you to wreck it by adding paint. I thought you were going to glaze," thinking it was partly my fault for suggesting he get back to the image. After a couple of hours it does look better, but sort of vague and generalized. It is a lot of paint. He gets away from it, and worries about the turtleneck for a while and then we quit. M says he will work on it before the next sitting.

§

§

THIRD SITTING

Again I arrive happy, tho not effusive. The studio is as before. My shoulder is killing me, but the pose does not over-tax it, and I am placed as before. M has worked on the painting, attacking the pink paint, subduing and modeling. The turtleneck is gone and I have that sort of clerical collar he uses so often to avoid both flesh and involved clothing. The image looks more like me, but has a weariness completely foreign to the Empire Builder we started from.

The radio has gone back inside the house, and I sit quietly and he paints quietly most of the time, getting into one fairly long discussion about the form of poetry. M paints rapidly, working on the neck of the clothes, and cleaning up the features, spending a good deal of time on the hair. I had not had a haircut in some time and it was very long. For the first time, a lock of hair falls across my forehead and he paints it in. The sittings seem longer, and the day is rather dingy.

The image softens and crumples, and I appear frightened of something in it. We look at it, and I sit on the couch watching him paint. We talk about Scientological matters and I get rather nervous about nothing. M picks it up immediately and wants to know what's wrong. "I don't know." We have dinner.

Dark and cold—in the studio afterwards. M paints some more, and finally it becomes impossible. He can't seem to get what he wants, and is projecting some very unpleasant image of me.

We sit down on the couch and look at the ptg and talk for about an hour. "How does it look to you?" "I look frightened, crumpled." "Where are you?" It takes a long time, but I work out a picture of me riding a bicycle across an empty space with a brick wall on one side and a big gate. "What are you afraid of?" I don't know, only that someone will frighten me, and I avoid looking at it, peddling my bicycle like mad to get out of there.

In the first version I looked very young. Here I look older, and M has even put some greyish highlights in the hair. But behind it all I look young. It is very withering. I am upset and nervous and we talk about it. M says this is how I appear without my glasses, and I could look this way to him because I am trying to see without them. Natural. He asks if I feel he has taken away my sight. I say no. "If that's the way I look to you," I say, "alright, that's the way I look. It's damn unpleasant, but I feel you're being honest, putting down what you see."

"Would you be able to live with the picture?" "Not right now, but I might be able to rationalize whatever it is that's troubling me in the picture and accept it."

We go inside and drink coffee. I tell M: "I don't think that's the way I am as a general rule, but it is an aspect, however distressing, of my personality. If you want to change it, with or without me there, OK. If you want to leave it, OK too." I express my trust.

§

FINAL NOTES

I have looked again at my portrait, and it is very dark, not brooding, but dark and full of inner tension. David Afraid and (I guess) impotent against "it."

I like it (can confront it) much better. It looks different now that it has dried.

Los Angeles 1962 revised Santa Barbara 1978

mirrors

Gary Livingston
Stanley Berne
Richard Kostelanetz
Sasha Newborn

Gary Livingston

Having personal experience with violence (conceiving, committing and controlling it), I like to think I have something useful to say on the matter. My first book, *Exile's End*—about a kid who shoots his parents and everyone surviving to become best of friends—was published in England by Tambimuttu, and in the U.S. by Sagarin Press of Sand Lake, NY, and otherwise ignored in both countries. After years of fretting welfare and menial jobs, I'm now circulating an outline for a sequel to this true story.

My poetry and fiction has appeared in *New American Poetry* (McGraw-Hill), *The Virginia Quarterly Review, The Expatriate Review, The Little Magazine, The Smith, Quixote*, etc., with recent acceptances on brotherhood and/or violence in *The Smith* and *Brooklyn Heights Press.*

How To Avoid Killing Someone

1. *Let someone else do it.*

Small consolation that it is, it's good to know that someone else will not only share my worst urges, but will probably beat me to the punch. My most practical vicarious experience is reading about mass murder over the shoulder of a fellow straphanger. I always know someone else will illuminate my rage. Everyone is born borderline, and it's a relief to know that some will lose their passports long before I have a chance to test the virtues of freedom.

Without fail, every grim Justice I've imagined has been surpassed by some less optimistic Other. For every no-hostages situation I sketch, someone else is sure to eclipse Manson, Son of Sam and Vietnam. For every abbatoir I blueprint, some Sullivan is sure to crowd the sky, and so much the better, because sometimes I can easily see me naked in court trying to justify my collection of newspaper clippings.

"Because I'm leaving clues to the apocalypse, your Honor, in case I die."

I can see my eyes burning into some judge's before he
sentences me to life after a thousandth of a second of a glance. I
can see me losing all night at poker and calling it luck. I can see
me getting acquainted with all the spaces in my cell. I can see my
plea degenerating into unspeakable demons, and the padded room
Thorazine can't soften. I can see beauty as a once-attainable ideal, an
alternative I had no faith in; and I'm glad to know that someone else
who doesn't see these things will lead the way.

2. *You don't have to die to get attention.*

There are few things more satisfying than walking into a psychiatric
emergency ward and announcing you are going to kill everyone in
sight. Or asking for a lobotomy. The attention—or lack of attention—
available voluntarily is every bit as gratifying as that obtained
outrageously.

The use of shrinks and mental-health technicians as whipping
posts is well-documented in the annals of witchcraft. Experience is
obviously a better teacher of human sciences than the academy, and
it's easy to hate Them, if only for their incomes. No reason to be
cowed by power; just fake the tests, good and crazy, and take a rest. A
fair voluntary trial before deciding violence is worthwhile can save a
lot of trouble.

In an institution you quickly learn there's no such thing as
dignity. You learn that people really do kick you when you're down,
and if the story's hot, profit. You learn that your wife was better than
your bank account, your brother better than your banker and your
parents saints, and that the number of options on the Outside may
have been obscene, but no reason to be uptight.

Institutions are shaped by the administrator's notion of relevant
social values. A wrath-of-God warden will encourage a wrath-of-God
ward; pathologically medieval as he may be, there'll be no release
without an embracing of chivalry. A benevolent-despot institution
is characterized by a superior ability to abuse truth, to view the
honest inmate as polluted with truth. There are hypocritically liberal
institutions, known for publicizing the substitution of drugs for
chains, and insidiously permissive institutions, giving more than
enough rope for the eager recidivist.

Ultimately, institutions are hard to get out of because few of their
captains care. No matter how profound or true your story, policy calls
it sick. You're there; as a volunteer or with money, you might get out.
If nothing else, a voluntary excursion of society's healing archipelago

might inspire a thought process which eventually suggested freedom as the best means to credibility.

3. *Cultivate safeguards against despair.*

One of my best defenses against violence is having accomplished a number of unknown but noteworthy works while young, before becoming so demoralized that happiness somehow involved mowing down rows of editors.

I wrote an epic book while still believing there were people of taste who believed in the advancement of merit; I wrote another book, then made it a novella, and completed another 20 or 30 stories to round out one long or two short collections. I have hundreds of poems. Some of this work has even been published by respectable, if weak, references, and I know if someone asks what I've done with my life, I can keep him busy for a long time. If someone determines I'm a failure because my work's no good, I can show him official reviews that imply excellence, and state my earned right to choose critics. I always have at least one book handy for immediate publication should the climate change, and have great reservations about trying to change it prematurely by violence.

The road to violence is often paved with good intentions. The more tangible those intentions, the more demonstrable, the easier it is to maintain a wait-and-see attitude. Beneath the sameness of days and apparent immutability of the Rut is the security that change has more chances than the lottery. If outstanding effort often goes unrewarded, it can always be viewed as insurance against the day when you'll be standing there with a smoking gun, listening to witnesses heap belated praise.

With perfected talent, at best life can be like waiting for a cancer cure. With no awareness of talent, it's possible for an attitude alone to work: that society will get what it deserves; there's no shortage of frustration. It's possible to go around utterly torn between love and murder and somehow act in the best interests of humanity, because it's better to be rejected for being beautiful than for being ugly.

4. *It's not you, it's It!*

In the Russian science-fiction epic *Solaris*, there's a scene where an astroshrink is told by one of the few remaining scientists aboard a station orbiting a sentient sun that if anything weird happened, like dead nightmares materializing, it was because of a pissed-off star. Ever since bombarding its surface with X-rays in an effort to stimulate conversation, strange things had been happening on the station, like the disappearance of the crew.

Lately, psychiatrists have been debating the impact of the news, whether or not there is some pattern of imitation to the rash of murders and suicides that follow publicized violence.

"From the few that I have examined, I have never seen a situation where the murderer was at least consciously prompted by news or knowledge of other murders," one prominent shrink was quoted in the papers. The next day, the papers reported, "In a letter to Station KAKE-TV, Wichita's B.T.K. Strangler asks, 'How many do I have to kill before I get a name in the paper or some national attention? One little paragraph would have been enough…"

Hijackers and other maddogs often claim higher motives; they did it for the good of the world, they did it for their children. They did it because something was wrong with a world that didn't otherwise reward them.

I've come to believe that the quintessential experience of insanity is feeling you have more to offer than you're allowed to give, of wallowing in the developmental impasse between what you're doing and what you should be doing. Insanity is merely the difference between potential and reality, the choice between doing bullshit or going nuts.

The Loser who happens upon various news items and puts two and two together but is told the best way to a better life is to vote is sure to suffer. Experts are paid well to explain violent phenomena to the wellpaid. Experts who represent the essence of social order become shrinks, and enjoy the irony of treating people who are retreating in extreme from that order.

In an era when it's possible to believe that one's loftiest dreams are definable as dangerous symptoms, when those things society regards as sick often represent the healthiest aspirations of our species and there's a preoccupation with suicide, it's sometimes necessary to believe that truth is hostility and hostility is truth, but actual violence ultimately the path to oblivion. Though bad news sells papers, and many unworthy people seem to prosper, there's no reason to believe that there are no good people, that it isn't rewarding to be good, that humanity has no exploitable instincts other than the urge to watch accidents.

While the tendency has been to complicate the definition of good, to equate it with fitting a certain mold, to believe it is many things in addition to violence, a society where marriage was illegal and cohabitation saintly, with legal drugs and illegal health foods, with black leaders and white bleeders and everything upsidedown would feel exactly the same as it does today; it would be as easy to get arrested. Crime would still start at the top and be perpetuated by bigshots buying violence to keep the junkies, cops, lovers, pornographers, nosepickers and idealists in place, and violence would remain the only immoral constant worth incarcerating.

The best people have never had a sustained and credible chance to test tenacious standards; the best art, acting and sentiment has been murdered or driven to murder, the best leaders murdered, the best environments murdered and plundered. It becomes incumbent upon the Loser to prove he's worthy of being left alone, because They are always checking, always trying to flush out the antisocial elements, and for all practical purposes it's better to assume that the hassle and loneliness results more from being one of the best, rather than worst, of cogs, and that while the burden might indeed be on society to provide a break, it is incumbent upon the Loser to know that and not flip out, because the best people never quite kill.

Stanley Berne

Born in Staten Island, NY; son of William (a businessman)
and Irene (Daniels) Berne; married Arlene Zekowski (writer
and university professor). Eastern New Mexico University,
Portales, associate professor of English. Military service: US
Army Air Forces 1942-1945; served in South Pacific theater;
received Philipppine Liberation Medal. Writings—all published
by Wittenborn, except as noted: (with wife, Arlene Zekowski)
A First Book of the Neo-Narrative; (with Arlene Zekowski)
*Cardinals and Saints; The Dialogues; The Multiple Modern Gods and
Other Stories; The Unconscious Victorious and Other Stories; The
New Rubaiyat of Stanley Berne* (poetry), American-Canadian
Publishers; Work represented in anthology, *Breakthrough
Fictioneers,* edited by Richard Kostelanetz, Something Else
Press, 1973.

from The Great American Empire

After all, the death of a man is of so little moment to a world filled
with people. There might even be some relief, if a stranger, in the
knowledge that now there was room for one more.

He had always suggested that cremation was the best way, clean,
the ground was after all so cold, the ants that build tunnels would
come upon the flesh. Did they carry it away in those small morsels
that they carry before them to their warrens and there store it until
the cold, the winter, and then did they feed upon it? That was it. That
was why he did not care for the ground as burial, better like a hero,
an old hero, Beowulf upon the pyre, the mourners in a circle; but, of
course, his possessions would not be burned with the body.

His brother snickered and elbowed his wife, his own, a coarse
shallow one dimension, eye on material such as a dress, a relative
who might leave them money, children that she brought forth, one of
her own from an earlier marriage. She always rather misunderstood
and secretly despised the scholarly victim, the deceased, because she
was like so many in the city, a vulgar shining attractiveness so that
wiping the mouth of her child she bent over in a short skirt revealing

starkly white underpants, also very short, clean, with a lace edging at the brown thigh, a thigh tanned in the sun, bent over purposely so he could see it and he saw it but somehow the attraction of the sight was only 25% of what it ordinarily ought to be, and there was then nothing wrong with his senses, that is, at 45 he had still been both attractive and attracted.

The vogue for hair was well on then, before the next phase of shaving, shaving of the shagpot, so to speak, the scalp now carefully cut and shaved and polished, both men and women, the whiskers gone, sideburns, moustaches, even eyebrows, for both sexes, smooth as billiard balls and very smart and modern indeed, quite suitable to the people whose style of life had brought them colonies on the moon and on Mars and one of the things that got in the way of simple hygiene on the planets was hair, and so it had to go, since both sexes were going and coming and you couldn't put all that hair in a helmet.

But he was now missing all that, lying still, smiling, with a beard Vandyke style, the old sideburns to the bottom of the lobe of the ears, the moustache still heavy and blond extending within an inch of the sideburns, he had been a man with a sense of dignity, a man of letters, of the old school who had accomplished the modest, it always seemed to him, accumulation of five published volumes of a new combination, new in those days, of prose and poetry which a newspaper critic in a Dallas paper dubbed the "Neo- Narrative." And that was his small contribution to the world. That is what he had left, and not very many people had ever heard his name, read his books, knew or cared for a new combination at all, and still less did they value the thought that energized that which he had spent his life forming, forming, indeed, with a hope born of a struggling youth that somehow life could be made richer by freeing the feelings of the post-Victorian era in which he had grown up.

It was America in the 1920's that had formed those hopes, indeed "ideals" that he had dreamed of and been nurtured upon as a boy, a long time ago. That window out of which he looked, barred against illegal entry, that air even then permeated by soft lead, the smell of a new pencil, the soot that fell three times a day from burning incinerators.

He determined that discipline alone would carry him to success, a success that was a dream, a world tiny and round with an irregular surface, the clouds of atmosphere that surrounded the greenery of a globe lost in space yet a prisoner of regularity, of form and law, the law of spinning and turning, the law of distance from the sun, the law of energy that emitted the golden touch of life, light, heat, the law that informed the fabric of the earth itself, the water, crystal clean, cool, that bubbled from the heat of the earth's core that over the centuries had cooled and warmed life into bodies and brains and organs that had penetrated as did his ancestors, the caves, the rocks, the nights, the penises, the clitorises, by the millions of pounds of seed and energy that slowly rose by law, the demand met of supply and hunger that had finally evolved a creature of the 1920's sitting at a window of a slowly disintegrating city, writing poetry. Man is a poetry writing animal, indeed.

But nothing would succeed, nothing he could do about his inheritance, blond hair, blue eyes, a large nose, sensitive lips, a well formed chest, large, manly, thin hips and legs, short really, five feet six inches.

The hope of a life is the dream such as led him of leaving that house, that window, those bars (on the window), that air, that odor, of leaving his body which he wrestled with as a prisoner in a cell, that cell that body which occupied that moment of time, that chair before the desk, that desk before that accursed window, that door through which he walked to his bed and to her as he waited for her downstairs in the street.

Why was she late? What kept her? She was always late. He could hardly wait.

Still a poet, the youth and energy of his body, a boy of 23 demanded that connection, warmth, sympathy, contact of touching which thundered at him through the loins, the legs that twined round her, the arms crushing and pulling her to him, the want and need of a thirsty man crossing the desert in a merciless cruel July sun that burned down and dried out the tongue and gums until to drink seems the greatest pleasure, and so to drink of her, at 23 as they mounted the stairs, the confidence of possession and pleasure just minutes away, her breasts and founts and entry and penetration and relief and swallow and breathe as she lay upon the white sheets, white, black hair on the pillow and poetry and woman seemed quite one, so strong was his belief in himself as a poet, and now confirmed by the experience and reward of her, that in his body he was a man.

Very few people attended the funeral. There was his father, now almost ninety, still hearty, his brother and his brother's wife and both of them came gaily to the burial because (1) they were still alive and well, (2) they were burying him, (3) he died unknown, as they preferred, and (4) now that he was dead, all of Father's fortune would descend on themselves and their children. He was the main obstacle in the way of their inherited fortunes. And the one good friend and his wife and their two children, the friend and the one friend he had managed to retain from his friendship-making days, those days of seventeen, the very height of friendship, the time to make friends is when you can give all to a friend, all your time and energy and attention, all your worldly goods,' (since you have no possessions or entailments it is quite easy) and all your shared dreams in which you and your friend are active and equal partners.

And those were all who came.

Richard Kostelanetz

Life Story
by Richard Kostelanetz
Music of Today (Time-Life Records, 1967)
The Theatre of Mixed Means (The Dial Press, 1968; Pitman [London], 1970)
Master Minds (Macmillan, 1968; Rodolfo alonso Editor [Buenos Aires], 1972)
Visual Language (Assembling Press, 1970)
In the Beginning (Abyss [Somerville, MA], 1971)
I Articulations / Short Fictions (Kulchur Foundation, 1974)
Recyclings: Vol. 1, 1959-67 (Assembling Press, 1974)
The End of Intelligent Writing (Sheed & Ward, 1974)
Openings & Closings (D'Arc, 1975)
Portraits from Memory (Ardis, 1975)
Constructs (WCPR [Reno, NV], 1975)
Modulations (Assembling Press, 1975)
Extrapolate (Cookie Press [Des Moines, IA], 1975).
Rain Rains Rain (Assembling Press, 1976).
Illuminations (Laughing Bear, 1977).
One Night Stood (Future Press, 1977).
Foreshortenings (Tuumba [Berkeley, CA], 1978).
Constructs Two (Membrane [Milwaukee, WI], 1978).
"The End" Appendix (Pentagram [Milwaukee, WI], 1978).
Twenties in the Sixties (Assembling, 1978).
Metamorphosis in the Arts (Abrams, forthcoming)
[As Author]

The New American Arts (Horizon Press, 1965; Bibliografica Omeba [Buenos Aires], 1967; Lidador [Rio de Janeiro], 1967)
[As Co-author and Editor]

On Contemporary Literature (Avon, 1964; Books for Libraries, 1971; revised edition, Avon, 1969).
Twelve from the Sixties (Dell, 1967).
The Young American Writers (Funk & Wagnalls, 1967).
Beyond Left & Right (Morrow, 1968; Diamond [Tokyo], 1974).
Imaged Words & Worded Images (Outerbridge, 1970).
Possibilities of Poetry (Dell, 1970).

Moholy-Nagy (Praeger, 1970; Allen Lane-Penguin, 1971).
John Cage (Praeger, 1970; Allen Lane-Penguin, 1971).
Social Speculations (Morrow, 1971).
Human Alternatives (Morrow, 1971).
Future's Fictions (Panache [Princeton, NJ], 1971).
Seeing Through Shuck (Ballantine, 1972).
Breakthrough Fictioneers (Something Else, 1973).
The Edge of Adaptation (PrenticeHall, 1973).
Language & Structure (Kensington Arts [Toronto], 1975).
Essaying Essays (Out of London Press, 1975).
Younger Critics in North America (Margins/Tom Montag, 1976).
Esthetics Contemporary (Prometheus, 1978).
　　　　　[As Editor, with critical introductions]

Assembling (Assembling Press, 1970),
Second Assembling (1971),
Third Assembling (1972),
Fourth Assembling (1973),
Fifth Assembling (1974),
Sixth Assembling (1975),
Seventh Assembling (1977).
　　　　　[As Co-Compiler, with polemical prefaces]

Text-Sound Art in North America, ABC of Contemporary
　　Reading, Reincarnations, Plus/Minus, And So Forth, Intermix,
　　Polyartistry.
　　　　　[Unpublished books]

Richard Kostelanetz (b. 1940, New York, NY) is a full-time writer.

Autochronology

> Autobiography is only to be trusted when it
> reveals something disgraceful.—*George Orwell*,
> "Some Notes on Salvador Dali" (1944).

1940　Born in New York, New York, 14 May, the day Holland fell
　　　to advancing Germans (and Emma Goldman died). Son of
　　　Boris, an immigrant lawyer, and Ethel, a sometime organizer-
　　　publicist.

1941　Declaration of official U. S. involvement in WWII.

1944   Impresses adults with arithmetical tricks, mostly involving calendar dates and days of the week.

1945   End of WWII. Franklin D. Roosevelt dies. Father commutes to a "war frauds" job in Washington.

1946   He returns to New York to open private practice. Beginnings of the post-WWII prosperity.

1947   Matriculates at Downtown Community School, which leaves warmer memories than subsequent, more prominent educational institutions.

1948   Israel's independence, 14 May.

1950   The globe falling at Times Square precisely divides the twentieth century. .

1951   Unfortunate removal to a Westchester suburb-detached houses with lawns on an approximate grid of streets.

1952   Election of Dwight D. Eisenhower and the ascendancy of his cultural tone. "Conformity" becomes not a social choice but a behavioral imperative.

1953   Learns to read Hebrew in six months; forgets it totally one month later.

1954   Decides writing should be his profession. Mother refuses parental permission to play school football.

1956   All-State High School Choir, conducted by William Dawson of Tuskegee Institute; sole experience on stage of applause that is more than gratuitous.

1957   Sees first Mondrian paintings and is haunted by them. Nearly thrown out of Scarsdale High School for organizing an imagined insurrection. Eagle scout.

1958   Eager departure to Brown University, Providence.

1959   Learns to like reading and sex, and to do both abundantly. Cures teenage insomnia by reading into the early mornings and then sleeping to noon. To avoid departments of English and "Creative Writing," both of which seem deleterious, decides to major in "American Civilization"; a Frenchman, met at Knossos, jokes, "It is a short course." Sees the Living Theatre's production of *The Connection*, and reads Ralph Ellison's *Invisible Man*, both of which remain in the head.

1960   Election of John F. Kennedy and temporary ascendancy of his cultural style. Meets S. Foster Damon, Brown's noted Blakist, who teaches not how to write but how to be a writer; there is a crucial difference. Moves off-campus. Meets Bunny.

1961   Initial publication in a national magazine. Reads Edmund Wilson, Henry Miller and Norman O. Brown. Learns of Ad Reinhardt. Co-edits an off-campus literary magazine and then is nearly expelled from college for publishing a colleague's putative pornography. Studies accounting at father's insistence at Columbia University summer school, in addition to essay writing. Drops accounting after two classes, but continues writing, beneficially.

1962   Rejects military draft at Columbia graduate school. Considers Harvard and Yale but cannot accept their morning classes. Woodrow Wilson Fellowship in history, in spite of erratic grades. Returns to New York. Fortunate marriage.

1963   First of the devastating political assassinations. Discovers Bach through his *Passions*. Also the musics of Charles Ives and John Cage. Publishes prose in periodicals. Scores first book contracts.

1964   Fulbright scholarship, King's College, University of London. Briefly studies harmony and music composition. Beginnings of Vietnam War and LBJ prosperity. The first of several pioneering anthologies.

1965   Nearly bounced from the Fulbright program for provoking the chief administrator's envy. Glad return to New York. Resolves never to leave home again for so long and won't, for more than two weeks, for the next decade. Fortunate dissolution of marriage. Publishes critical analysis of U.S. literary politics that inspires virulent reactions, if not professional excommunication. Produces filmed portraits of U.S. artists for BBC. Pulitzer Fellowship in critical writing, for studies in the non-literary arts.

1966   M.A., American history. Journalistic profiles of Marshall

McLuhan, Milton Babbitt, John Cage and Herman Kahn, among others, who collectively become a second, different, better graduate school. Reads Moholy-Nagy's *Vision in Motion* for the first of many times. Hears interminable lecture by Buckminster Fuller, who redefines radical politics. Moves to East Village, forsaking academia for bohemia, revamping my perspective on New York and its culture; new apartment is six blocks south of Downtown Community School and one mile east of Boris and Ethel. Meets Julianne.

1967 Surprised to receive Guggenheim Fellowship—the last grant for almost a decade. Admires hippiedom from a close distance, but spurns drugs stronger than grass. Decides not to marry again so soon. Writes first poems worth preserving. Ad Reinhardt dies.

1968 Flunks pre-orals for a Ph.D. and unequivocably retires from graduate school; Columbia's loss is my gain. Signs national advertisement for Bobby Kennedy in May; distraught in June. Disgusted with Democratic convention, but votes against Dick Nixon as worse than Dick Daley. Initial "illuminated demonstrations" of visual poetry, projected on slides against a voice-over narration, and initial publication, in both magazines and anthologies, of my creative work. Begins verbally minimal fictions. Inclusion in *Who's Who in America* (incredibly) and *Directory of American Scholars* as an historian (credibly). Ascendancy of Richard M. Nixon and subsequent economic and cultural demoralizations.

1969 Publishes *Master Minds*, potentially a very popular book; but the sick-slick publisher blows it. Begins visual fiction and drafts first prophetic, much-reprinted manifesto. Rediscovers swimming, mostly in the Saugatuck River. Earns money. Americans land on the moon on television. Completes *Metamorphosis in the Arts*, which is soon set in type but remains needlessly unpublished for several years. Vows to overcome reclusive life-style. Meets Queenie.

1970 Publication of several books: criticism, anthologies, creative work, recapitulating interests of the previous decade. Commences "The Maturity of American Thought," a comprehensive intellectual history, which is put aside in November to draft *The End of Intelligent Writing* in three heated months. Co-founds Assembling, a counter-authoritarian publishing experiment, giving hundreds of contributors more creative freedom than they have had before (or since). Discovers the professional potential of small literary book publishers.

1971   Persistent vain attempt to find a publisher for *The End*. Friends have no better luck. Nothing much happens.

1972   Distressed by the suppression of *The End*, considers alternative professions-consulting, advertising, night-watching. The engaging optimism of the McGovern nomination and his supporters is quickly squelched along with so much else that showed promise in the seventies. Accepts first adult job, teaching arts to policemen. Overcomes fears of public-speaking. Begins numerical art. Visits Jerusalem.

1973   Uncovers over a dozen unpublished books in files. Demoralized. Drafts "ABC of Contemporary Reading," which typically takes years to get into public print.

1974   Belated appearance of *The End*, to mostly favorable notice, though some prominent media disgrace themselves with compromised reviewers. Commercial powerhouses black-list, or black-talk, and refuse to paperback it, interest notwithstanding. From now on, publishes books strictly with small presses, as much by necessity as choice. Relishes Nixon's departure. Writes and narrates "Poetry To See & Poetry To Hear," Camera Three, CBS network. First silk-screened prints. Assimilates Theo van Doesburg. Objects to precious obscurities in "Art." Drafts *Recyclings*, consciously regurgitating earlier writings for a different future. Moves with Sytske to Soho, de-emphasizing Literature for Art.

1975   First one-man New York exhibition. First sales of visual art. Draws prolifically. Makes initial audiotapes and then videotapes, adding new arts without abandoning old ones. Appearance of several volumes of creative work; few reviews. Discovers that *The End* sticks in readers' heads; reissued. Guest-curator, "Language & Structure," traveling exhibition. Recognition as an "artist," sort of.

1976   Envisions "Wordsand," a retrospective of creative work in all media. Visits Mount Sinai, the beginnings of Western civilization, and then the Basel Art Fair, the end. Makes first films and firstphotolinens. Stages sexti-media presentation of Openings & Closings, 330 one-sentence stories. Votes reservedly for Jimmy Carter. Meets Mary again.

1977   Teaches in Austin, Texas, leaving New York for eight consecutive weeks, and then four and three more, missing a brutal winter.

Sasha Newborn

Born in Mason City, Iowa, 1940, first memory WAR ENDS, I could read age 5. Two years at MIT taught me not to be an engineer, University of Iowa, first job Peace Corps teaching in Tanzania taught me not to be a teacher. Floating through the Sixties as activist, editor of *Middle Earth,* an "underground newspaper" in Iowa City. Five years knocking about New York City, temp jobs at publishers taught me the insides of publishing. Santa Barbara, typesetter in a print shop designing Black Sparrow books, left time to launch poetry press, then edge into college publishing.

from The Basement

My first night in the basement, I'd found a man on the mattress he had a raincoat on, it was Stash. He'd woken unnoticeably, as a snake's transparent eyelids unnoticeably open.

he didn't say anything but got up to leave he was as if always leaving and now he was leaving, one of the brightest when I'd first seen him

I'd thought he was a kid, now he didn't look different but he was not a kid, he had been dealing, high-priced shoplifting, swindles, bad bargains—the dark eyes hiding many details but not hiding the person he'd become.

Too bright not to cheat, he cheated at living, he cheated the sidewalk when he moved almost shuffling in his thick raincoat, he cheated the cold of the nights he slept in cars, he cheated the words out of his mouth

the waves in his soft hair, his large ears and forward nose kept the impression of youth like a mask in front of him. I felt he was capable of anything, and that was his power.

Now he got up and in the shadows went out the door and noiselessly up the stairs, only the magazines would be left in the morning.

raunchy big city mags, the specialized market of slut smut glut, the girls disappointing in newsprint halftones on gray pages in too many or too few clothes—taste lacking, thought lacking, edges of

pages worn thin with wrinkles from thumbs. these were jackoff bad jackoff mags on the dusty cement floor, round spots of dirt of scum of cum as thick as the dirt-crusted basement window panes. Summer was over and we were all on the long coast down from the full sun to weak days, short days, and the night inside becomes what we are.

We are animals, we scurry for shelter. In the morning, I moved box after box across downtown through the alley the shortest way and down the storm cellar stairs to the basement.

Expensive to live in this country. I'd lived on less than nothing in Africa & traveling—currents were different now, indefinably shifted, the old comfortable connections no longer held.

this was nearly three years later.

I held the beer can against my cheek, feeling through my beard the cold, but still not believing—not sure that reality itself was real.

these were head days, lived on the philosophies of dissolute French poets and of hardheaded mule-stubborn experiment: to live each day for itself, to ignore money, to write, to think, to live—if this wasn't real, what was?

What I wanted was to die floating above conversations, descend into the Pit and feel all the sensations possible to man and then to die.

and die again and be afraid and be everything and nothing, a dust, an orange, a bolt, but alive, aware, knowing it, conscious of myself, and to be that and to dream.

story

Charles Bukowski
Morty Sklar
James Brown

Charles Bukowski

Charles Bukowski was born in Germany and raised in Los Angeles. He published his first short story in 1944, and in the Sixties wrote a column "Notes of a Dirty Old Man" for *Open City* newspaper. He has over twenty books to his credit, most of them translated. This selection is from his forthcoming novel *Women* (Black Sparrow, fall 1978).

from Women

We came in low over Kansas City, the pilot said the temperature was 20 degrees, and there I was in my thin California sports coat and shirt, lightweight pants, summer stockings, and holes in my shoes. As we landed and taxied toward the ramp everybody was reaching for overcoats, gloves, hats, mufflers. I let them all get off and then climbed down the portable stairway. There was Frenchy leaning against a building and waiting. Frenchy taught drama and collected books, mostly mine. "Welcome to Kansas Shitty, Chinaski!" he said cheerfully and handed me a bottle of tequila. I took a good gulp and followed him into the parking lot. I had no baggage, just a portfolio of poems. The car was warm and pleasant and we passed the bottle.

The roadways were frozen over with ice.

"Not everybody can drive on this fucking kind of ice," said Frenchy. "You got to know what you're doing."

I opened the portfolio and began reading Frenchy a love poem Lydia had handed me at the airport:

"...your purple cock curved like a..."

"...when I squeeze your pimples, bullets of pus like sperm..."

"Oh SHIT!" hollered Frenchy. The car went into a spin. Frenchy worked at the steering wheel.

"Frenchy," I said, lifting the tequila bottle and taking a hit, "we're not going to make it."

We spun off the road and into a three foot ditch which divided the highway. I handed him the bottle.

We got out of the car and climbed out of the ditch. We thumbed passing cars, sharing what was left of the bottle. Finally a car stopped.

A man in his mid-twenties, drunk, was at the wheel. "Where you fellows going?"

"A poetry reading," said Frenchy.

"A poetry reading?"

"Yeah, at the University."

"All right, get in."

He was a liquor salesman. The back seat of his car was packed with cases of beer.

"Have a beer," he said, "and get me one too."

He got us there. We drove right up into the campus center and parked on the lawn in front of the auditorium. We were only 15 minutes late. I got out, felt nervous, vomited, then we all walked in together. We had stopped for a pint of vodka to get me through the reading.

I read about 20 minutes, then put the poems down. I felt hostile. "This shit bores me," I said, "let's just talk to each other."

I ended up screaming things at the audience and they screamed back at me. That audience wasn't bad. They were doing it for free. After about another 30 minutes a couple of professors got me out of there. "We've got a room for you, Chinaski," one of them said, "in the women's dormitory."

"In the women's dorm?"

"That's right," he said gently, "a nice room."

...It was true. Up on the third floor. One of the profs had brought a fifth of whiskey. Another gave me a check for the reading, plus airfare, and we sat around and drank the whiskey and talked. I blacked out. When I came to, everybody was gone and there was half a fifth left. I sat there drinking and thinking, hey, you're Chinaski, Chinaski the legend. You've got an image. Now you're in the women's dorm. Hundreds of women in this place, *hundreds* of them.

All I had on were my shorts and stockings. I walked out into the hall up to the nearest door. I knocked.

"Hey, I'm Henry Chinaski, the immortal writer! Open up! I wanna show you something!"

I heard the girls giggling.

"O. K. now," I said, "how many of you are in there? 2? 3? It doesn't matter. I can handle 3! No problem! Hear me? Open up! I have this HUGE purple thing! Listen, I'll beat on the door with it!"

I took my fist and beat on the door. They kept giggling.

"So. You're not going to let Chinaski in, eh? Well, FUCK you!"

I tried the next door. "Hey, girls! This is the best poet of the last

18 hundred years! Open the door! I'm gonna show you something!
Sweet meat for your vaginal lips!"

I tried the next door.

I tried all the doors on that floor and then I walked down the
stairway and worked all the doors on the second floor and then all
the doors on the first. I had the whiskey with me and I got tired.
It seemed like hours since I had left my room. I drank as I walked
along. No luck.

I had forgotten where my room was, which floor it was on. All
I wanted, finally, was to get back to my room. I tried all the doors
again, this time silently, very conscious of my shorts and stockings.
No luck. "The greatest men are the most alone."

Back on the third floor I twisted a doorknob and the door opened.
There was my portfolio of poems...the empty drinking glasses,
ashtrays full of cigarette stubs...my pants, my shirt, my shoes, my
coat. It was a wonderful sight. I closed the door, sat down on the bed
and finished the bottle of whiskey that I had been carrying with me.
Then I gratefully lay down.

I awakened. It was daylight. I was in a strange clean place with
two beds, drapes, t.v., bath. It appeared to be a motel room. I got up
and opened the door. There was snow and ice out there. I closed the
door and looked around. There was no explanation. I had no idea
where I was. I was terribly hung over and depressed. I reached for the
telephone and placed a long distance call to Lydia in Los Angeles.

"Baby, I don't know where I am!"

"I thought you went to Kansas City?"

"I did. But now I don't know where I am, you understand? I
opened the door and looked and there's nothing but frozen roads, ice,
snow!"

"Where were you staying?"

"Last thing I remember I had a room in the women's dorm."

"Well, you probably made an ass out of yourself and they moved
you to a motel. Don't worry. Somebody will show up and take you to
the airport."

"But why didn't they leave a note?"

"Just relax. Lay down or take a shower. Somebody will show up
to take care of you."

"Christ, don't you have any sympathy for my situation?"

"You made an ass out of yourself. You generally always make an ass out of yourself."

"What do you mean 'generally always'?"

"You're just a lousy drunk," Lydia said. "Take a warm shower."
She hung up.

I walked over to the bed and stretched out. It was a nice motel
room but it lacked character. I'd be damned if I'd take a shower. I
thought of turning on the t.v. I slept finally...

There was a knock on the door. Two bright young college boys stood
there, ready to take me to the airport, just as Lydia had predicted. I
sat on the edge of the bed putting on my shoes. "We got time for a
couple at the airport bar before take-off?" I asked.

"Sure, Mr. Chinaski," one of them said, "anything you want."

"O.K." I said. "Then let's get the fuck out of here."

I got back, made love to Lydia several times, got in a fight with
her, and left L.A. International late one morning to give a reading
in Arkansas. I was lucky enough to have a seat by myself. The
flight captain announced himself, if I heard correctly, as Captain
Winehead. When the stewardess came by I ordered a drink.

I was certain I knew one of the stewardesses. She lived in Long
Beach, had read some of my books, had written me a letter enclosing
her photo and phone number. I recognized her from the photo. I had
never gotten around to meeting her but I called her a number of times
and one drunken night we had screamed at each other over the phone.

She stood up front trying not to notice me as I stared at her
behind and her calves and her breasts.

We had lunch, saw the Game of the Week, the after-lunch wine
burned my throat, and I ordered two Bloody Marys.

When we got to Arkansas I transfered to a small two engine job.
When the propellers started up the wings began to vibrate and shake.
They looked like they might fall off. We lifted off and the stewardess
asked if anybody wanted a drink. By then we all needed one. She,
staggered and wobbled up and down the aisle selling drinks. Then
she said, loudly, "DRINK UP! WE'RE GOING TO LAND!" We
drank up and landed. Fifteen minutes later we were up again. The
stewardess asked if anybody wanted a drink. By then we all needed
one. Then she said, loudly, "DRINK UP! WE'RE GOING TO
LAND!"

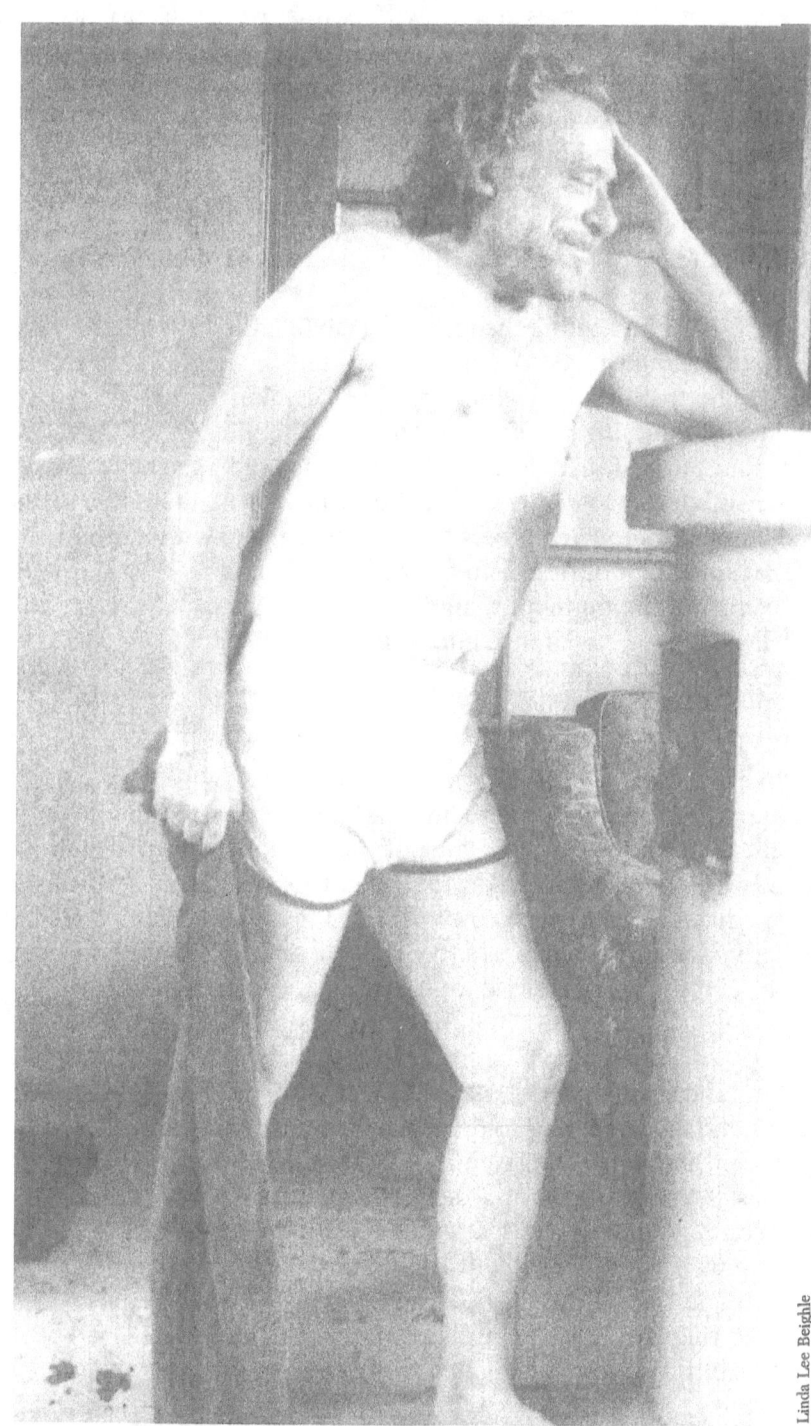

Professor Peter James and his wife, Selma, were there to meet me. Selma looked like a movie starlet but with much more class.

"You're looking great," said Pete.

"Your wife's looking great."

"You've got two hours before the reading."

Pete drove to their place. It was a split-level house with the guestroom on the lower level. I was shown my bedroom, downstairs. "You want to eat?" Pete asked. "No, I feel like I'm going to vomit." We went upstairs.

Backstage, just before the reading, Pete filled a water pitcher with vodka and orange juice. "An old woman runs the readings. She'd cream in her panties if she knew you were drinking. She's a nice old girl but she still thinks poetry is about sunsets and doves in flight."

I went out and read. S.R.O. The luck was holding. They were like any other audience: they didn't know how to handle some of the good poems, and during others they laughed at the wrong times. I kept reading and pouring from the water pitcher.

"What's that you're drinking?"

"This," I said, "is orange juice mixed with life."

"Do you have a girlfriend?"

"I'm a virgin."

"Why did you seek to become a writer?"

"Next question, please."

I read some more. I told them I had flown in with Captain Winehead and had seen the Game of the Week. I told them that when I was in good spiritual shape I ate off one dish and then washed it immediately. I read some more poems. I read poems until the water pitcher was empty. Then I told them the reading was over. There was a bit of autographing and we went to a party at Pete's house...

I did my Indian dance, my Belly dance and my Broken-Ass-in-the-Wind dance. It's hard to drink when you dance. And it's hard to dance when you drink. Pete knew what he was doing. He had couches and chairs lined up to separate the dancers from the drinkers. Each could go their own way without bothering the other.

Pete walked up. He looked around the room at the women. "Which one do you want?" he asked.

"Is it that easy?"

"It's just southern hospitality."

There was one I had noticed, older than the others, with protruding teeth. But her teeth protruded perfectly—pushing the lips out like an open passionate flower. I wanted my mouth on that mouth. She wore a short skirt and her pantyhose revealed good legs that kept crossing and uncrossing as she laughed and drank and tugged at her skirt which would just not stay down. I sat next to her. "I'm..." I started to say..."

"I know who you are. I was at your reading."

"Thanks. I'd like to eat your pussy. I've gotten pretty good at it. I'll drive you crazy."

"What do you think of Allen Ginsberg?"

"Look, don't get me off the track. I want your mouth, your legs, your ass."

"All right," she said. "See you soon. I'm in the bedroom downstairs."

I got up, left her, had another drink. A young guy—at least 6 feet 6 inches tall and mean looking—walked up to me. "Look, Chinaski, I don't believe all that shit about you living on skidrow and knowing all the dope dealers, pimps, whores, junkies, horseplayers, fighters and drunks..."

"It's partly true."

"Bullshit," he said and walked off. A literary critic.

Then a cute blonde, about 19, with rimless glasses and a wide smile walked up. The smile never left. "I want to fuck you," she said. "It's your face."

"What about my face?"

"It's magnificent. I want to destroy your face with my cunt."

"It might be the other way around,"

"Don't bet on it."

"You're right. Cunts are indestructible." I went back to the couch and started playing with the legs of the one with the short skirt and moist flower lips whose name was Lillian.

The party ended and I went downstairs with Lilly. We undressed and sat propped against the pillows drinking vodka and vodka mix. There was a radio and the radio played. Lilly told me that she had worked for years to put her husband through college and then when he had gotten his professorship he had divorced her.

"That's tacky," I said.

"You been married?"

"Yes."

"What happened?"

" 'Mental cruelty,' according to the divorce papers."

"Was it true?" she asked.

"Of course: both ways."

I kissed Lilly. It was as good as I had imagined it would be. The flower mouth was open. We clasped, I sucked on her teeth. We broke.

"I think you," she said, looking at me with wide and beautiful eyes, "are one of the two or three best writers of today."

I switched off the bed lamp fast. I kissed her some more, played with her breasts and body, then went down on her. I was drunk, but I think I did O.K. But after that I couldn't do it the other way. I rode and rode and rode. I was hard but I couldn't come. Finally I rolled off exhausted and went to sleep...

In the morning Lilly was flat on her back, snoring. I went to the bathroom, pissed, brushed my teeth and washed my face. Then I crawled back into bed. I turned her toward me and started playing with her parts. I am always very horny when hungover—not horny to eat but horny to blast. Fucking was the best cure for hangovers. It got all the parts ticking again. Her breath was so bad that I didn't want the flower mouth. I mounted. She gave a small groan. For me, it was very good. I don't think I gave her more than twenty strokes before I came.

After a while I heard her get up and walk to the bathroom. Lillian. By the time she came back I had turned my back to her and was nearly asleep.

After 15 minutes she slipped quietly out of bed and began to dress.

"What's wrong?" I asked, not turning over.

"I've got to get out of here. I've got to take my kids to school."

Lillian gently closed the door and ran up the stairway.

I got up, walked to the bathroom, and stared for a while at my face in the mirror.

At ten a.m. I went upstairs for breakfast. I found Pete and Selma. Selma looked great. How did one earn a Selma? The dogs of this world never ended up with a Selma. Dogs ended up with dogs. Selma served us breakfast. She was beautiful and one man owned her, a college professor. That was not quite right, somehow. Educated hotshot smoothies. Education was the new god, and educated men the new plantation masters.

"It was a damned good breakfast," I told them.

"Thanks much."

"How was Lilly?" Pete asked.

"Lilly was very good."

"You've got to read again tonight, you know. It'll be at a smaller college, more conservative." He didn't look at me.

"All right. I'll be careful."

"What are you going to read?"

"Old stuff, I guess."

We finished our coffee and walked into the front room and sat down. The phone rang, Pete answered, talked, then turned to me. "Guy from the local paper wants to interview you. What'll I tell him?"

"Tell him all right."

Pete relayed the answer, then walked over and picked up my latest book and a pen. "I thought you might want to write something in this for Lilly."

I opened the book to the title page. "Dear Lilly," I wrote. "You will always be part of my life...

Henry Chinaski."

Morty Sklar

Morty Sklar was born in New York City, lived there most of
his life, and came to Iowa City via the 1971 National Poetry
Festival in Michigan and the words of a person he'd met there:
"Iowa City is a nice place to live."
Morty is editor/publisher of The Spirit That Moves Us Press
which last year brought out *The Actualist Anthology,* and is
currently putting together *Editors' Choice: an Anthology of
Literature & Graphics from the U.S. Small Press, 1965-1977.*

from Getting Up

> *"Maan, I got to get up from this baad muthafucker!"*
> *—junkie waiting in a hotel room on West 47th Street*
> *in New York City, 1963.*

Roger and I bought some of Ilma' s dope and got off right there in
her kitchen, the three of us sitting at the porcelain top table. A rare
moment, for me, being with a friend I loved and a woman I loved.
And along with Ilma's being poor and in a ghetto with her child, and
without a mate and the windows facing a courtyard around which
was nothing but the rear of other tenements surrounding poverty's
garden of garbage and unwanted bedsprings and mattresses, burnt
out TV'S, those rotten, mildewed perennials wafting in on a summer
breeze, with Ilma *herself* throwing garbage sacks out the window and
my feeling futile at the thought of telling her "Ilma, you shouldn't,"
and feeling futile about so much else and therefore not saying
anything, thus arriving by the strangest route to that place I found
myself again that night, acceptance. Of everything. Of nothing.

The kitchen window offered a larger view with distance between
the buildings and sky, so that it attained a kind of grandeur—a New
World ruins. If it was lovely, that was because it was real.

The front window was on Madison, where Ilma's "stereo" and

TV were, but where she spent the least time. A hundred feet from it ran the New Haven-Hartford Railroad, time-machining people from downtown where the money is made, to the northern suburbs of New York and to Connecticut, carrying in each window the profile of a person about as aware of us as a TV image would be, or maybe just watching our reality pass.

Our reality. Some call what I've been describing unreal. But Roger's and Ilma's and my sharing of it was real, and that is what kept us going.

Ilma was a good connection because she was a good person and because I could go to her house to score. That meant for me, little exposure to junkies and police on the street. And she wasn't a user herself, neither did she have junkies hang out in her home—except for me of course, and Roger. But the quality of her dope, which was fair to start with, became poor and poorer. At 101 East 122nd Street or somewhere else on the street, if I took my time I could score shit that was twice as good as hers, but most street connections were good only for a few days at a time. Also, the ones with the best dope were plagued by beat artists who waited for people to come and score and then took their stuff afterwrds, or took their money beforehand.

I was stealing more. But I felt I needed to give Klein's a rest before I was a-rest-*ed*, so I hit Korvette's.

Korette's was great because there were several of them around town, all with the same merchandise and basic store layout. In the one on 34th Street in the downtown departmentstore district, there were London Fog raincoats/topcoats. They were a terrific bargain at $20—which is what I asked for when I took them to individuals rather than pawnshops which offered only twelve. It was so easy that I took orders for size and color, *then* stole them. So easy I had to stop myself because how long could I keep it up? So I switched temporarily to slacks—good ones which brought only 3 or 4 bucks at the pawnee's but of which I stole a couple or three at a time. I'd take several into a dressingroom, look at one in front of the mirrors in salesmen's presence, then go back to the dressingroom and drape two or three over a belt I wore outside the waist loops and covered them with my coat, then returned the other pair to the rack.

One Friday night Ilma had halfloads: 15 threedollar bags for 25 bucks. I had only ten bucks. Roger was working but had only a buck and a half in tops and he already spent an advance of his evening's pay. I asked Ilma for two bags out of a halfload in advance and said I'd pay her later that night.

It was eight o'clock. I was feeling too comfortable in Korvette's downtown and that made me less alert, but it was the only Korvette's open til 10pm. Klein's late nights were Tuesday and Thursday. I thought about Alexander's uptown on the eastside but I was already downtown. After I got this halfload, I figured I could maybe get by a little while reselling.

Weren't many people shopping.

My favorite pants rack was one where I could see a surveillance camera fifty feet away, but which couldn't see me from the waist down. I draped three pairs of pants over my arm so that they looked like one. If you wanted to really play it safe when you stole from a departmentstore in New York City you would pay attention to: each shopper no matter how harmless looking, everything you ever heard people talk about, regarding store security, like TV, buttons sewn into garments which triggered an alarm when the garment was carried thru a street door—and on and on. But if you did all that you probably would decide to not steal anything because business is in the business of staying in business and a junkie is just out to feed his habit. And when you think about being professional like the business people, you realize that the effort, discipline and commitment it requires could be better put to use quitting junk and doing something constructive, safer and with a sense of continuity. Why spend all your energies being a junkie when you really want to be a writer? a human being? And how could you do your best anyhow, if you didn't believe in what you were doing? And what would ultimate success be?—the attainment of a lifetime supply of junk? The achievement in life of not having to live?

I scored and was on the way to the Sixth Avenue exit without a sound of footsteps behind and no one in my periphery vision.

I walked up Sixth toward the subway, getting nearer to that mystical border defined by psyche, experience, luck and ritual which tells you you're safe. I crossed the avenue at 35th so that if anyone was following I might see them cross too. I didn't see anyone. It wasn't until he was several feet behind and speaking so casually that I thought he was asking directions, that I saw the man. From across the street, another, who could have been a construction foreman judging by his clothes, fixed on our coordinates. The right thing seemed to be for me to surrender.

James Brown

I have had no recent publications, save *Going Fast*, but my
short stories have appeared in *Tales* ("Sonny Said Goodbye"),
Samisdat ("What I Did Over My Summer Vacation"), etc.
Presently I'm working on another novel.

from Going Fast

It was a good party. Gloria came and we had a chance to talk. It was
a short but good talk.

Louie, Frank, Dave and Bret and their girls came. Manual and a
bunch of his friends came and they brought their girls—small, tight
lipped girls with suspicious eyes. And the friends of all these friends
came. We even invited the college students who lived below us, and
they agreed to let us use their stereo for the night, though actually
we didn't need music. People danced without it. There was lots of
smoke. It stung my eyes. Lots of wine. Beer too. JT and me, during
the party, ran out with Manual for a pony keg of Coors, and when we
got back, the flat was even more crammed. We could hardly move.
Ten s'cuse me's to five steps. Word got around fast. I'd say there were
at least forty people sitting and standing around our place, drinking
wine and beer and smiling. The line to the bathroom was ridiculous.
You either had to wait forever or go outside against the wall of Bobby
Brown's.

Cars to the party nearly filled the block. People drifted in from
every direction and the only way we could tell if they belonged
at our party was if they were young and friendly. That's all we
cared about. The bums and halfways from Winchell's, who saw
the commotion, kept trying to stop people for a little money or a
cigarette or something, and they would size up the incoming girls,
occasionally pawing at them as an excuse to get attention. They
said some obnoxious and embarrassing things, too. They almost
ruined the party. It got out of hand when about ten bums sat down
ad blocked the porch steps, and when we caught one of them in the
party pocketing bottles of wine, that was it and Manual had to help

out. The bums fought over a bottle as they wandered into the streets, taking their time as if to say, "We got dignity; you punks don't scare us." But they left like beaten dogs. Tensed. Cautious. We were young; they were old. JT, me, and Manual went back upstairs. I listened to the different people talk, always standing a little outside the circles. The college students had taken to a corner to chat about seminars and the pass-fail system at DC Santa Cruz. It was boring. The bad asses talked in Spanish so I couldn't understand them. Some jocks, dressed in plaid slacks, talked about football as they demonstrated different blocking techniques. I listened to them all. Then I went to the kitchen for some more beer. People sat on the edge of the sink, flicking their ashes into the drain. Guys had cornered girls to talk softly to them. When I left the kitchen things in the other rooms were getting more frantic and loose. But it was for the better. People, drunker and less uptight, broke from their cliques and started speaking freely from one person to another. This wasn't only amazing, it was great. It helped restore my faith in people.

Music shook the walls and dancing thundered the floor. We played Jerry Jeff Walker; Bruce Springsteen; and much to my dislike, Led Zepplin. I don't like hard rock too much. But I was too drunk to really care.

Some people sat on the window sills, while still others teetered across to Bobby Brown's roof to wave at the passing cars. People came and went. The door to our apartment was open. Big Manual stood just outside the crowded hallway near the stairs, guzzling from a half-gallon pitcher of beer and, finishing it, foam dripping from the corners of his mouth, he let out this tremendous "Yeehaw," followed by five or six less powerful "Yeehaws," and like it was a calling of sorts, JT in drunken playfulness and coming from nowhere I could see, flew through the air and landed on Manual's back, bronco style.

"Hot damn, giddyup,"

Manual gagged on his belly of beer, and stunned and knocked off guard, slipped on a step with JT still riding him tight like a tick on a dog's neck. Manual grabbed the handrail but it pulled right out of the wall and they both went falling, cussing and tumbling down the stairs making an earthquake. When they hit bottom they sat there on the floor dazed and shaking their heads, and then Manual came out of it and reached for JT and JT beat it up the stairs again with Manual hot ass after him. But just before JT got to the top Big Manual took a football dive and got hold of his ankle.

"Help, Virg, help!"

JT clutched the doorway for life. Manual tugged. I thought if JT didn't let go soon his leg was going to pull right off like that handrail did, but he was stubborn and fighting like a cat held over water. He didn't want to go. It was hard to tell if they were just funning.

"Help, Virg, help!"

I thought about it. In a last effort, as JT was being peeled loose, he grabbed this guy's pant leg and this other guy tried shaking loose but he couldn't, and when he felt himself going he grabbed the belt of this other guy, and that last guy on the chain held tight to the doorjambs with both hands as long as he could while Manual backed down the stairs, pulling, panting, straining and saying, "Ya sonsabitches, ya sonsabitches," till I'd finished thinking and decided what the hell?—so I took a leap through the narrow stairway and when they saw me about to land right on all their heads, Manual let go and they ducked and we all went snowballing down those stairs, knocking out the banister spokes, snap, snap, snap, smashing against the walls and busting the plaster, screaming "Ahhhhhh" and cussing as our bodies, a jumbled maze of limbs, picked up speed and an innocent person coming up the stairs for that fantastic whirlwind rumbling, rumbling crash through the screen door to a bruising finale on the porch. I was on the bottom.

"Oh," I said, "Ohhhh."

Three knees in my back, an elbow in my eye. Slowly, ever so slowly, all those arms and legs and faces began dismantling, totally ignoring what they were stepping on in the process. I lay spread-eagled on the cold porch with my face pushed in, and finally, when the weight was off me and I could move, I looked up. Gloria looked down. Her pretty face was blank.

"Virgil?"

I didn't know what to say. I know I didn't look good, since I must have gotten scroungy going down those stairs. I felt a sweaty coolness on my back telling me my shirt was ripped there. Everybody ran up to the party, laughing like crazies again, leaving the two of us alone. There was silence. Then she held out her hand to help me up and we both started laughing. We went upstairs for some wine.

Lots of people complimented me on my daringness and great fall, and I soaked it all up feeling like a genuine rowdy, which I'm not. Little Big Virgil. Man of the Great Stair Tumble. But walking into that party with Gloria beside me made me feel even better. Compared to all the teeny-boppers, Gloria stood out. I told her I'd be right back and then I went to the kitchen for two iced Ronald McDonald glasses. That's all we had. We got them with a cheeseburger.

Jenny sat in the kitchen by herself with her boot up on the table, drinking her self-brought bottle of Spanada and eyeing JT meanly as he pivoted against the refrigerator kissing another girl. JT took his hand out of her blouse when I opened the freezer and a cold mist floated into their faces.

"Gonna get in trouble, bub."

"Don'tcha worry." JT smiled. The girl looked at me curiously. He pulled her head around to him again. JT was right. It was none of my damn business. Besides, I was too caught up feeling proud about Gloria to care what he did. I was holding a bottle of 1959 Cabernet Sauvignon. Humph! Humph!

I hurried back to Gloria.

"A gift from a friend of JT's father," I said.

She could see I was lying, since there must have been twenty raunchily dressed rowdies around us drinking vintage wines out of the bottle as if it were Red Mountain or something. The music, which had been turned off for a while, went back on and it was too loud to talk, so we just sat there sipping wine and staring at each other. I hate loud music. But it was still nice just sitting there and watching her, and I felt pretty content for a while. But soon I wanted to talk a little. I wanted to ask her if she wanted to go outside for a walk, but each song break when it was quiet enough to speak, I couldn't quite get the nerve to say what I wanted. For one thing, it would have sounded awfully much like a pick-up line to let's-go-out-and-neck, and that wasn't what I had in mind. Honestly. Of course I wanted to kiss her, but really, I didn't have any plans to make a move on her. I just wanted to be alone with her. I just wanted some cool air because I was a little too drunk and I needed to sober up so I wouldn't say anything dumb. I wanted things to be right, and—there's not much of anything worse than trying to carry on a conversation with a drunk person when you're not drunk. I know I hate that. I could laugh at everything that wouldn't seem funny to a sober person, and I know a sober person could laugh at things a drunk person would never laugh at. I didn't want Gloria to be uneasy. So I decided I must ask her if she wanted to go outside, but at the same time I asked, 1'd be honest about it by saying—Now, I don't mean this as a pick-up Gloria, I want you to get that straight so you won't be offended or anything. Honestly, Gloria.

The stereo went through the mechanics of dropping another record and I had to hurry. "Gloria." She perked up and looked me in the eyes. Christ, that nearly killed me! "You want to...ummmm...I mean I was...."

"Huh?"

"Well, first of all I don't want you..."

"What're you trying to say, Virgil?"

The record dropped and the arm moved.

"I was thinking maybe..."

"Yes?"

I felt like I was proposing or something.

"Maybe we could...Oh hell. Do you want to go outside?"

She laughed. "Why not?"

The music played.

"It's too loud in here," I hollered.

She agreed, nodding.

Gloria put her sweater on. It was made of thick bleached wool and had Mexican embroidery around the waistline where a thin sash hung, which she tied gently and firmly in a bow, pulling the sweater against her body in a way loose enough to be comfortable yet tight enough so that you could see the outline of her waist flaring down to her plump, round hips. She moved down the stairs and she moved nice. I know a lot of people say that women are either glorified or condemned, and nobody ever looks at the real woman. That's a bunch of crap. I don't like to see anybody condemned, but when a woman is beautiful, I don't see a damn thing wrong in admiring her. Beauty is a real part of a woman, and you can't separate it from the woman herself because it has a lot to do with how she thinks. I like pretty women. It's the ugly ones that are bitching. When we stepped out on the porch, I knew I was looking at someone very real and very pretty. She pulled the collars of her sweater up about her neck. Her nose was a little pink. She looked extremely cuddleable. We didn't walk. We sat close together on the stairs and sipped our wine, shivering and looking across the vacant street. The light from a lamp was a hazy yellow in the mist. Strands of Gloria's hair curled slightly, neatly and naturally from the moisture. You could hear music and the clamoring of people above us, but it was faint, so we weren't bothered. I took a deep breath and felt better, feeling the good heat of her thigh light against mine. She wrapped her arms about herself. Her lips quivered and she shook her hair back. Her lobes were pink. She smiled. I held, her. We laughed a little and I was happy then. She was no threat. How could she be? I wasn't scared any more. Whatever happened, whatever resulted from this night, I was willing to roll right along with it, because there was, I thought, no reason not to. We didn't say much. There didn't seem to be a reason for or against that either. What could have been silent, uneasy moments were instead, good moments. Whether that was because I was a little drunk and less uptight, I don't know, but I know I felt more at ease and free than I'd ever felt with her before—which isn't saying much as I'd only met her once before. But none of that mattered to me now.

We drank and I filled her glass again.

"I'll have to be leaving soon," she said.

"You just got here an hour ago."

"I have to get up early for school tomorrow."

"School?"

"Yes, school."

"But the party..."

"I didn't come for the party, Virgil, I came to see you."

When she said that, everything was better.

She leaned her head forward to look at me, "You understand, don't you?"

"Well, it's late, but you're at least going to finish your wine first, aren't you?"

"Of course." And we laughed a little again and she stayed a while longer, her nose getting pinker and my eyes growing smaller, trying to feel out exactly how she thought of me, The pressure building in me was a good one. I held her tighter. Of course I didn't want her to go, but I thought it would be all right if that's what she had to do. I thought I'd see her again, soon.

"Friday. Maybe Friday we could see a movie or something together. The El Rey is showing all the old Flash Gordon's and they're really, really funny. Or maybe there's something else you want to do?"

She thought for a moment like I figured she would, not wanting me to think her too anxious in accepting. Something like that, something I knew she'd eventually grow out of, I felt confident because I knew her pause was just sort of a ploy.

"Sure," she said. "I hear they're good."

"Friday?"

"Friday."

So I walked her to her Volkswagen and I had a date and we kissed; we kissed and I felt great. I felt I was about to have a relationship worth having, something I never had before. This was the start, I thought. I watched her drive off, turn a corner and disappear.

Then I started laughing. I laughed because I was thinking of how she kissed me, Not that it wasn't a good kiss; I laughed at myself because I'd never been kissed before by anybody I cared for. Sure, I've been kissed on the cheek by old ladies and fat aunts, but that doesn't count. I was laughing because I had just experienced a real mouth-to-mouth kiss. I was laughing because I caught myself feeling like one of those teeny-boppers who get a peck by some rock star. It was funny. I was dazed. Then I went back to the party to enjoy a better and different euphoric drunkenness for a few more short hours. Friday, Friday, Friday is how I'd look, Friday is how she'd look. Friday was movements and gestures and words and expressions all rolled into one as we strutted side by side, hand in hand, into the El Rey to see Flash Gordon. Friday, Friday, Friday.

I led the last straggler out about 4:00 AM and though there was a big messy job to be done, everything except the stairway hall was pretty much intact considering all the people who were there. The stereo receiver was on and I turned it off. I glanced around. Tomorrow, tomorrow. It could all wait till then. JT, though he vowed he'd score tonight and had warned me not to wake him in the morning because he'd for sure be in bed with somebody, was out by himself on Bobby Brown's with his feet up on the ledge, tilted in his chair and staring absently at the stars overhead. I leaned out the window.

"Good party, man. Got me a date Friday with Gloria."

"Yeh?" He stretched and yawned. "My, how people change. Ya did better 'an me, honcho. Yep, good party; yep, good party. Ya comin' out here or not? Okeydoke then, bring another of them bottles with ya, buddy."

I looked around the kitchen. Everything could be cleaned tomorrow. No use getting frantic now. I got another bottle. My head still wandered with Gloria and Friday night. Friday night. I climbed out the window. I was tired but it was a contented tiredness, and I could have slept but I wanted to stay up and take advantage of the good feelings.

www.ingramcontent.com/pod-product-compliance
Lightning Source LLC
Chambersburg PA
CBHW050950120626
46552CB00001B/476